# i can cook

## from the garden

## grow, cook and eat with Katy

recipes by Sally Brown & Kate Morris
gardening by Martyn Cox

hamlyn

An Hachette UK Company
www.hachette.co.uk

First published in Great Britain in 2012 by
Hamlyn, a division of Octopus Publishing Group Ltd
Endeavour House
189 Shaftesbury Avenue
London
WC2H 8JY
www.octopusbooks.co.uk

ISBN 978-0-600-62406-6

A CIP catalogue record for this book is available from the British Library

Printed and bound in China

10 9 8 7 6 5 4 3 2 1

i can cook logo © Endemol UK Limited 2009.
i can cook is a trade mark of Endemol UK Limited. i can cook is
produced by Initial (part of Endemol UK Limited) for the BBC
BBC and BBC logo are trademarks of the British Broadcasting
Corporation and are used under license.  BBC logo © BBC 1996

Series Consultants and Co-Devisers: Kate Morris and Sally Brown
Recipes by Kate Morris and Sally Brown
Gardening text by Martyn Cox

## Notes

Standard level spoon measures are used in all recipes:
1 tablespoon = one 15 ml spoon
1 teaspoon = one 5 ml spoon

Ovens should be preheated to the specified temperature. If using a
fan-assisted oven, follow the manufacturer's instructions for adjusting
the time and temperature.

We recognise that many parents are choosing to avoid nuts and nut
products so most of the recipes in this selection do not include nuts (or
they may be added as an optional extra). Always be aware that
ingredients may have nut traces in them so check the packaging for
allergens if there is a risk of an allergic reaction.

## About the authors

**Sally Brown** After a successful career in corporate PR & marketing,
including driving the profitable launch of a B2C US Corporation in the
UK, Sally took time away from her career to raise her family. With a
passion for cooking combined with the belief that young children can
achieve and learn so much more from cooking than parents realise
(her two young daughters at the time were clear evidence), Sally
launched The Purple Kitchen Company in 2000. Committed to building
an authentic business, Sally welcomed Kate Morris to the company
and focused on delivering innovative cooking classes for children from
the age of 2 years old. Sally is married with two teenage daughters.
Her parents were caterers and food retailers.

**Kate Morris** After initially qualifying as a Home Economics teacher and
spending 2 years at a secondary school in North London, Kate moved
into consumer education. Kate first worked for a home interest
monthly national magazine for over 3 years (*Woman and Home*) and
then continued to work freelance for a further 10 years. Kate has
extended her technical knowledge, qualifications and understanding
of the power of food education in young children's lives both through
the practical teaching with Purple Kitchen over the past 9 years and
further study with an OU certificate in Human Nutrition (2007) and her
recently completed MSc in Food Policy from City University, London
(2010). Kate is a Fellow of the Royal Society for the Promotion of Health.

**Martyn Cox** Martyn trained in horticulture and is the author of many
gardening books, including *Gardening with Kids* and *RHS Wildlife
Garden*. He is gardening columnist at the *Mail on Sunday* and has a
small, plant-packed garden in East London which he shares with his
partner and two young children.

# Contents

Foreword 6

Introduction 7

i can Garden 12

i can cook Lunch 48

i can cook Tea 78

i can cook Sweet things 102

Index 126

Acknowledgements 128

# Foreword

Welcome to our new book, *i can cook from the garden*. We had lots of fun putting it together and we hope you enjoy growing, cooking and eating all the delicious things in the book.

It's such fun making your own meals and even more special when you have picked and grown the ingredients. Imagine making your own vegetable tart with squishy squashy tomatoes you have grown; or picking your own juicy strawberries and putting them in a strawberry meringue pudding. Sowing your seeds, watering them, watching the plants grow and then harvesting your vegetables, or digging them up out of the ground, is really rewarding.

You will find out here how to grow easy-peasy vegetables, herbs and fruit. And don't worry if you don't have a garden. There are lots of lovely things you can grow in pots on window ledges and in little spaces such as a balcony. And it's not just about the plants. Because it's nice being outside in the fresh air we have also put in the book ideas for other things to make and do – such as colourful potato-print pictures or helpful mini-beasts you can spot in your plants.

We have given you 35 delicious i can cook recipes which you can really cook yourself. Here and there you may need to ask an adult to help you but they have been designed specifically for you to enjoy making and eating with friends and to share with your family. How exciting is that?

**Katy Ashworth**

# Introduction

Hello there. We all know that children like to cook for themselves, rather than simply watch an adult or help out with the preparation, but what's even more satisfying for them is when they can also grow some of the ingredients themselves. In this book we've selected some of the easiest-to-grow vegetables, fruit and herbs which children can harvest and use in the 35 tasty recipes, from main meals to healthy snacks to sweet treats.

## Little green fingers

If you thought you might need a large garden to grow your own, well, it's time to think again. All of the plants we've picked for this book, from strawberries to salad leaves, and from blueberries to carrots, can be grown in pots, making them ideal for any size of garden, whether you're lucky enough to own a big plot or simply have a patio or balcony. There are even some plants in this book that can be grown on a window ledge.

All of the plants are easy to grow and can either be started from ready-grown plants, which are widely available from garden centres, nurseries and DIY superstores, or nurtured from scratch by sowing seeds. While ready-grown plants will save you lots of time and are a good choice if you forget to sow seeds at the right time, raising plants from seed is cheaper and can be more rewarding for young gardeners – it's magical for them to place the seeds in the ground with their own hands, see them develop into plants and eventually harvest the leaves, pick the fruit or dig up the underground roots.

Showing children how to grow and look after plants for the first time will introduce them to a fascinating pastime that might grip them for life – but don't expect them to turn into green-fingered experts overnight! Grown-up gardeners are often very meticulous in the way they sow seeds, neatly prune plants or rake the soil until it is perfectly flat, but it's important to allow children to garden their own way, only offering some gentle guidance when they need it. Little hands are unable to sow seeds as precisely as adults or to water plants as accurately as someone who has done it for years, so try not to intervene too much. The plants will still grow and children will enjoy the responsibility of looking after them, rather than feeling as though the adult has done everything for them.

## Beyond the garden

Although most edible plants are available to buy in shops all year round, growing their own will help to teach children about the seasonality of food and where the food we usually buy wrapped in plastic from a supermarket really comes from. Gardening with children is a great way to develop their knowledge of wildlife and provide a gentle science lesson on many subjects, including what plants need to grow, how insects pollinate plants, along with the difference between annuals and perennials.

## Tools

You do not need many tools to grow great things to eat. The ones you will use the most are:
* a hand trowel
* a hand fork
* a spade
* a rake
* a watering can

If you have a larger garden, a wheelbarrow can be useful. Rather than using adult tools which are too big for little hands, buy smaller ones that have been specially made for children.

## What to wear

Everyone gets dirty when they do some gardening. Either put a gardening apron on your child to keep their clothes clean, or leave their best clothes indoors and have them wear old things that they are allowed to get muddy. A pair of rubber boots to wear when digging will keep shoes clean.

## Safety first

Growing activities or spending time in the garden is great fun, but there are a few things to be aware of to keep children safe.

* Apart from fruit and vegetables, many other plants in the garden may have attractive berries. Most of these shouldn't be eaten, so explain that they should only pick things to eat when you are with them.

* Hands should always be washed thoroughly after handling soil, compost, plants or even just playing in the garden.

* Children's tools usually have blunt edges, but they should still be used with care. Keep sharp secateurs or gardening knives away from children and explain why you have to use some of these cutting tools for the time being. Children can use scissors to prune soft stemmed plants or to harvest some vegetables, fruit, herbs or edible flowers. Make sure they use these scissors only for gardening!

* Make sure they wear boots or shoes when digging to prevent accidents.

* Never let children handle fertiliser, weed killer or pesticides. Make sure these are beyond their reach and locked in a shed or garage.

* Take care with bamboo canes and try to buy ones that are long enough to be above head height when pushed into the ground. Hunt around the garden for old snail shells, paint them a bright colour then put on top of the pointed ends.

So, what are you waiting for? Snap up some seeds or plants, collect some pots, buy some compost and get your child growing. It's that simple. And before you know it your young chef will be proudly raising lots of their own ingredients.

## Little chefs

I can cook is all about children doing the food preparation and cooking themselves. Here and there they need to ask an adult for help, but most of the time they really are making delicious meals all on their own.

Here are a few hints and tips for you before you get started with your little chef.

**Work surface:** Make sure your child can stand to cook and has a preparation surface that is at the right height. Don't be tempted to let them stand on a chair to reach a higher surface as they might fall off. A picnic table, for example, can work well. On top of the work surface put a large work mat or chopping board to define the preparation area. You can then wash this mat thoroughly in very hot water.

**Apron:** It is a good idea to give children an apron to wear when cooking. This will protect your child's clothes.

**Grater:** A multi-purpose grater with suction pads to stick it to the work surface is a really useful thing to have. If you use another type of grater, be careful of little fingers.

**Scissors:** We recommend scissors rather than sharp knives to cut up everything from beans to bacon. Standard metal-bladed nursery scissors are great – and remember to use them only for food. If you teach your child our rhyme, they will get into good habits:

'Remember, when using scissors everyone knows, it's best to point them at your toes!'.

**Knives:** Keep sharp knives out of reach and out of sight and, when you do need to use a sharp knife, explain to your little chef why you have to do that bit for them.

**Scales:** With old-fashioned balance scales your little chef can actually see the pans levelling when the ingredients and the weights match.

**Spoons:** A teaspoon holds 5ml, a dessert-spoon holds 10ml and a tablespoon holds 15ml. Unless the recipe says otherwise, all our spoons are level.

**Cups:** This is the American measure. 1 cup = 250 ml.

**Mixing bowls:** We recommend 1 litre or 1.5 litre capacity.

**Keep things clean:** Encourage children to wash their hands and put an apron on before they start cooking and make the washing up part of the fun too.

### Techniques

The first time your little chef cooks something they might need quite a bit of help. But as they get used to the things they need to do, you will find they can do more and more themselves. Often they have used the same skills outside of cooking. Any child who can use a paintbrush can oil a baking sheet with a pastry brush, for example. Here is the explanation for some of the words and techniques we use:

**Breaking an egg:** Hold onto the handle of a cup with one hand and the egg with the other. Hit the egg on the edge of the cup and tap a few times. Listen to the sound change when the shell cracks. Then carefully use both thumbs to open the egg. Empty it into the cup.

**'Popping' a pepper:** Put a whole pepper on the work mat with the stalk facing up. Place both thumbs on the top where the stalk is, push down into the middle of the pepper and the pepper will 'pop'. Then pull it apart and remove the core and stalk.

**Tickling:** Rubbing butter and flour together between fingers and thumb to make a crumbly texture

**Tip and load:** This is when we measure liquids using a spoon. Put more liquid than you need into a jug or mug, then hold the handle with one hand and lift your elbow towards the ceiling, carefully tipping the jug.

Using your other hand, put the level spoon into the jug to fully 'load' the liquid on to the spoon. This ensures the correct quantity of liquid is used.

**Topping and tailing:** Taking the top and bottom off something like a green bean.

**The 'two spoon method':** We often use this for filling containers. Hold a spoon in each hand, then load some mixture on to one spoon and then use the back of the other spoon to push the mixture off.

**'Wet' and 'dry' bowls:** This is when we keep the wet ingredients like egg and milk in one mixing bowl and the dry ingredients such as flour and sugar in another mixing bowl.

### Hand-washing song

Hey everybody, it's time to wash your hands and get your aprons on.

Roll up your sleeves, give your hands a wash, with Slippy Dippy Soap, Splish Splash Splosh.

Cooking is fun but it can be mucky, So put your apron on to stop your clothes getting yucky.

Have you done your hands? **YES!**

Washed and dried? **YES!**

Sleeves rolled up? **YES!**

Apron Tied? **YES!**

**Let's take a look in the cookery book.**

**What can you do?**

**I can cook!**

# i can Garden

# Getting started

There are lots of different vegetables, fruit, herbs and plants with edible flowers that you can grow. Some grow really quickly and are ready for picking in just a few weeks, but others are much slower and take many months to grow, so you'll need to be patient!

### Be prepared!

Sowing seeds or planting plants in pots is easy, but some pots need preparing before you start. If your pot has lots of holes in the bottom to let water trickle out, all you need to do is add some compost. If your pot has just one hole in the centre, put pieces of broken clay pot or large stones over it to stop the hole from becoming full of compost.

### Sowing seeds

Seeds are amazing. Many plants grow quickly from seed and it's great fun watching seedlings appear from beneath the ground. After a seed has been sown, it soaks up the water beneath the ground and forms a root underneath that will hold

it in place. As the sun warms the soil, the seed then sends out a shoot that appears above the ground. Magic!

Most seedlings will appear within a week or two, so you won't have long to wait. Just fill a 7.5cm pot with seed compost, sow your seeds according to the packet instructions, then water the pot and place it on a sunny windowsill. After the seedlings start to grow, you may need to pull some up so the others have enough room to grow bigger.

## Growing plants

Most of the plants in this book need a warm, sunny spot to grow well, whether you are going to plant them in the ground or grow them in pots. It's best to avoid planting in shade unless you know the plant likes a shady spot.

## How fast do they grow?

### Very fast plants
Mixed salad leaves
Radish
Rocket
Basil
Spring onion
Nasturtium
Chives
Mint

### Fast plants
Runner bean
French bean
Broad bean
Tomato
Sweet pepper
Lettuce
Carrots
Courgette
Marigold

### Slow plants
Potato
Strawberry
Cucumber
Beetroot
Aubergine

### Very slow plants
Cauliflower
Cabbage
Brussels sprouts
Sweetcorn
Pumpkin
Apple
Pear
Raspberry
Apricot
Peach

## Watering

Plants get very thirsty, especially when it's warm and sunny. The best time to water them is in the morning or the evening, as plants prefer to be watered when it is not too hot.

Use a watering can with a sprinkler head on the end to gently water seedlings. If you don't put a sprinkler on, water will pour out too fast and wash away the compost and seeds. You can take the sprinkler off when the plants have started to grow.

Most plants will need a good drink once a day during summer, but some may need watering twice a day if they are covered in flowers or fruit. Plants in pots will get more thirsty than ones in the ground, so if you see some drooping stems or leaves, get out the watering can!

## Feeding

Just like us, plants need a healthy diet to grow well. If you grow plants in pots, there is usually enough good stuff in the compost to feed them, but some become really hungry when they are in flower or when the part you eat starts to grow. At this time they need to be given special plant food, sometimes every week. If you don't feed them, they will produce smaller fruit or vegetables, or just fewer of them. Ask an adult to add a few drops of plant food that is high in potash (which helps flowers and fruits to grow) to your watering can, so that the plants get the right amount. To make feeding easy, we have pointed out which plants have a really big appetite.

## Pesky pests

Not all mini-beasts are good. Some like to eat the leaves and fruit of the plants we are growing for food. Keep a close look out for pests and try to remove them by hand if you find any nibbling your plants. If plants are covered with pests, an adult may need to get rid of them by using an organic spray.

There are some things you can do to make plants less popular with pests. You can stick a band of copper tape around pots to stop slugs and snails crawling up the outside. You can also grow strongly scented herbs next to vegetables to put off some flying pests.

Don't worry if your plants are attacked, because if they have been fed and watered correctly and are growing in the right place, they should be healthy enough to recover.

## Wonderful wildlife

You'll spot many fascinating creatures when you spend time in the garden. Not only is it fun to watch them, but they are also good for your edible plants. Birds and even tiny mini-beasts, such as spiders, lacewings and ladybirds, gobble up lots of unhelpful creatures that eat our plants. Worms help to turn garden waste into compost and butterflies, and bees and even wasps help to pollinate flowers.

The flowers of some vegetables, fruit and herbs will attract these helpful creatures, but you will see more wildlife by finding space for bug boxes, bird tables or even by putting a big pile of stones or a few logs under a hedge – small animals and insects will take shelter inside.

# Magic name pot

Sowing your initial, name or making a pattern with seeds in a pot is great fun. Choose fast-growing plants and your design will magically appear above the compost within a week or so. If you have a long name or want to make a pattern, try using a seed tray. Make sure you sow shallow-rooted plants as these are not as deep as normal pots.

## When to do this

Spring    Summer

## What you will need:

- 30 cm pot
- multipurpose compost
- packet of fast-growing seeds, such as spring onions, radish, round rooted carrots, mixed salad leaves and chives
- pencil
- old colander or sieve
- watering can with rose head sprinkler

**1** Fill your flowerpot with compost, tickling any big lumps with your fingers to break them up and make the compost nice and smooth. Press down with your fingertips, so that there is a 5 cm gap between the compost and the top of the pot.

**2** Look on the seed packet to see how deep the seeds need to be planted. This is how deep your groove needs to be in the next step.

**3** 'Write' your initial or name in the compost by making a groove with the pencil. If you love drawing, add a pretty pattern, too. (It may help to draw your design on a piece of paper first, so you have a picture to copy.)

**4** Trickle your seeds carefully into the groove.

**5** Cover the seeds with compost. To do this, place a handful of compost in an old sieve or colander and shake it over the pot to break up any lumps. Water your pot carefully, then put it in a sunny spot.

### Looking after your pot
• Water the pot well and try not to let the compost dry out in warm weather.
• If the seedlings are squashed together, you may need to pull some out so the others have room to grow.

# Juicy strawberries

Grow a strawberry plant in a pot, put it in a sunny place and you can enjoy lots of juicy red, yellow or even white strawberries over summer. (And you thought they were always red…!)

**Plant**
Spring-Summer

**Flowers appear**
April to May

**Strawberries ready**
end of May to August

## What you will need:

- 20 cm hanging basket
- multipurpose compost
- trowel
- strawberry plant
- plant label and pencil
- watering can with rose head sprinkler

**1** Fill your hanging basket with compost, tickling any big lumps with your fingers to break them up and make the compost nice and smooth. Press down with your fingertips, so that there is a 5 cm gap between the compost and the top of the pot.

**2** Dig a hole in the centre of the basket with a trowel: it needs to be the same size as the little pot holding your strawberry plant.

### KATY SAYS

If you have a shady garden, you can grow tiny, but tasty Alpine strawberries.

**3** Slide the plant out of its pot, being careful not to damage the roots. Now place your plant gently in the hole. Pour more compost around the roots, then press down to keep the plant standing up straight.

**4** Press the top of the compost with your hand so it is nice and smooth. Write the name of the strawberry plant on a label and stick it in the basket or pot.

**5** Water the hanging basket using a sprinkler head so that the water comes out gently and evenly. Hang the basket in the sunniest spot you can find, so it gets lots of sun.

## Looking after strawberries

• Strawberry plants are very thirsty and like a lot to drink in hot, sunny weather.

• You'll get really big fruit if you feed plants once a week when they have flowers on them. Ask an adult to add a few drops of liquid tomato food to your watering can.

• After picking all the berries, use scissors to snip off the dying leaves to leave a clump of fresh leaves in the centre. Keep the plants damp, but not wet. In late autumn, put plants in a light, frost-free place, then put them back outdoors in spring.

## When to pick

Strawberries are ready to eat when they have turned bright red (or yellow or white…). If you can, pick them in the morning by pinching them off by the stalk. This helps the fruit to last longer and stops them from being squashed.

You can use your strawberries in Strawberry Crown (page 108) and Strawberry Meringue Pudding (page 118).

# Bursting blueberries

Dark blue, sweet-tasting blueberries grow on small bushes at the end of the summer. They need to be planted in ericaceous compost, rather than multipurpose compost.

**Plant**
March to May

**Flowers appear**
May to June

**Blueberries ready**
end of July to August

## What you will need:

- 45 cm pot
- soil-based ericaceous compost
- trowel
- blueberry plant
- plant label and pencil
- watering can with rose head sprinkler

**1** Fill your flowerpot with compost, tickling any big lumps with your fingers to break them up and make the compost nice and smooth. Press down with your fingertips, so that there is a 5 cm gap between the compost and the top of the pot.

**2** Dig a hole in the centre of the pot with a trowel: it needs to be the same size as the little pot holding your blueberry plant.

**3** Slide the plant out of its pot, being careful not to damage the roots. Now place your plant gently in the hole. Pour more compost around the roots, then press down to keep the plant standing up straight.

**4** Press the top of the compost with your hand so it is nice and smooth. Write the name of the blueberry plant on a label and stick it in the pot.

**5** Water the pot well with rainwater (blueberries love it!), using a sprinkler head so that the water comes out gently and evenly. Stand the pot in a sunny or lightly shaded spot, such as a window ledge or sheltered part of the garden.

## Looking after blueberries

- You will get lots of plump fruit if you feed plants every two weeks after the first flowers appear. Ask an adult to add some liquid fertiliser made for acid-loving plants to your watering can.
- The plants do not need lots of pruning, but ask an adult to snip off any untidy bits.
- Birds love blueberries too, so cover plants with garden netting as the fruit grows, or they might eat them all!

## When to pick

You can pick blueberries when they are plump, ripe, dark blue and slightly soft if you give them a gentle squeeze. Pull them off the branches of the plant with your fingers from mid- to late summer.

**KATY SAYS**

Blueberries are really good for you, as they are packed full of goodness.

# Tangy radish

These brightly coloured roots are great for snacks or salads and are really easy to grow. They come in red, pink, purple, black and white, so you can use them for a multicoloured salad.

**Sow seeds**
mid-March to mid-June

**Leaves appear**
March to June

**Radishes ready**
May to August

## What you will need:

- 30 cm pot
- multipurpose compost
- packet of radish seeds
- old colander or sieve
- plant label and pencil
- watering can with rose head sprinkler

**1** Fill your flowerpot with compost, tickling any big lumps with your fingers to break them up and make the compost nice and smooth. Press down with your fingertips, so that there is a 5 cm gap between the compost and the top of the pot.

**2** Carefully tear off a corner of the seed packet and shake a few seeds into the palm of your hand. Pinch a few seeds with your fingertips and scatter them thinly across the top of the compost. (Try to pick a still day, instead of a windy day, to do this!)

**3** The seeds need to be covered with fine compost to help them grow. To do this, place a handful of compost in an old sieve or colander and shake it over the pot to break up any lumps. Keep doing this until you have a layer 1.5 cm thick. Write the name of the plant on a label and push it into the pot.

**4** Water the pot well, using a sprinkler head so that the water comes out gently and evenly. Put the pot in the sunniest spot possible and water often in hot, sunny weather.

### KATY SAYS

Sow a new pot of radishes every two weeks or so to last you over the summer.

## Looking after radishes
• If your plants are squashed together in the pot, the radishes will be thin instead of plump and juicy, so gently pull up some seedlings to leave 2.5 cm between plants.

**When to pick** Radishes grow really quickly and are usually ready to pick four weeks after sowing. This means you have to keep an eye on them! Look at the plants every day and pull them up when they have reached the right size (check the seed packet for this). When you think they are ready, pull up one to test. If it is still too small, leave the rest to grow for a few more days, but try not to leave them in the pot for too long or they may become tough.

# Fantastic French beans

**Many bean plants grow really big, but French beans are smaller plants that are perfect in little spaces.**

**Sow seeds**
May to early July

**Flowers appear**
June

**Beans ready**
July to October

## What you will need:

- 45 cm pot
- multipurpose compost
- 5 bamboo canes (1.2 m long)
- garden twine
- packet of French bean seeds
- plant label and pencil
- watering can with rose head sprinkler
- soft twine

**1** Fill your flowerpot with compost, tickling any big lumps with your fingers to break them up and make the compost nice and smooth. Press down with your fingertips, so that there is a 5 cm gap between the compost and the top of the pot.

**KATY SAYS**

French beans are ideal as one of your five a day.

**2** French beans like to climb upwards, so make a bamboo wigwam in the pot. To do this, push the garden canes firmly into the compost, leaving the same-sized gap between each one. Gather the tops together and tie them together with twine. You'll need to ask an adult for help with this part.

**3** Use a pencil to make two 5 cm-deep holes at the bottom of each cane (one on either side) and pop a bean seed in each. Cover the seeds with compost. Write the name of the plant on a label and push it into the pot.

**4** Water the pot well, using a sprinkler head so that the water comes out gently and evenly. Put the pot in a sunny place.

**5** When the seedlings appear, remove the smallest of each pair, leaving the strongest one to grow.

**6** When the bean plants are about 15 cm tall, tie them to the canes with soft twine. As they grow, you will need to carry on tying the beans higher up until they reach the tops of the canes.

## Looking after French beans

• Water beans lightly while they are still small, keeping the compost just moist. Give them more to drink once the first flower buds appear.
• French beans are annuals (plants that live for only one year) and will die in autumn. When this happens, ask an adult to chop up the plants and add them to a compost bin.

**When to pick** You should be able to start picking your French beans about eight weeks after sowing. Snip off pods with a pair of scissors when they are large enough to eat. (Remember, 'when using scissors, everyone knows, it's best to point them at your toes'!) Picking the beans regularly while they are small and young will stop them becoming tough and will help new beans to grow.

You can use your beans in Baked Explorer Pancakes (page 68).

# Terrific tomatoes

Grow a tomato plant in a pot, and you will soon be picking masses of juicy sweet tomatoes. You can choose from bushy tomatoes (which hang down from their pot) or upright tomatoes (which need to be kept standing nice and straight).

**Plant**
late May to July

**Flowers appear**
May to June

**Tomatoes ready**
June to October

## What you will need:

- 30 cm flowerpot
- multipurpose compost
- trowel
- tomato plant (bought or grown from seed yourself)
- plant label and pencil
- watering can with rose head sprinkler

**1** Fill your flowerpot with compost, tickling any big lumps with your fingers to break them up and make the compost nice and smooth. Press down with your fingertips, so that there is a 5 cm gap between the compost and the top of the pot.

**2** Dig a hole in the centre of the pot with a trowel: it needs to be the same size as the little pot holding your tomato plant.

**3** Slide the tomato plant out of its pot. Be careful not to break the roots. Now place your plant gently in the hole. Pour more compost around the roots, then press down to keep the plant firm.

**4** Press the top of the compost with your hand so it is nice and smooth. Write the name of the tomato plant on a plastic label and stick it in the pot.

**5** Water the pot well, using a sprinkler head so that the water comes out gently and evenly. Stand the pot in the sunniest spot you can find. Tomatoes love the sun!

## Looking after tomatoes

• Water the tomatoes every day to keep the compost damp. If you use too much water the plants will become soggy and may die.

• Tomatoes don't need any food until they start to get flowers on them. Once you can see some flowers, ask an adult to add a few drops of liquid tomato food to your watering can once a week.

• If your tomato plant grows tall and needs help to keep it standing up straight, push a garden cane into the pot beside the main stem of the plant and tie the stem to the cane with soft twine. You may need to ask an adult to help you with this.

## When to pick

Tomatoes are ready to pick in late summer. Gently remove them, along with part of the green stalk – this helps them to stay fresh for longer.

You can use your tomatoes in Treasure Chest Tart (page 66), Pepper Boats (page 76) and Playtime Popovers (page 86).

Terrific tomatoes **29**

# Super-fast salad leaves

Packets of mixed salad leaves contain lettuce, mustard, rocket and other leafy plants, so you can grow a pot of leaves in many shapes, colours, textures and flavours. They grow really fast – sow some seeds and you will be picking lots of tasty leaves in just 3 weeks.

**Sow seeds**
mid-March to mid-June

**Leaves appear**
March to June

**Salad ready**
March to September

## What you will need:

- 20 cm pot
- multipurpose compost
- packet of mixed salad leaves
- old colander or sieve
- plant label and pencil
- watering can with rose head sprinkler

**1** Fill your flowerpot with compost, tickling any big lumps with your fingers to break them up and make the compost nice and smooth. Press down with your fingertips, so that there is a 5 cm gap between the compost and the top of the pot.

**2** Carefully tear off a corner of the seed packet and shake a few seeds into the palm of your hand. Pinch a few seeds with your fingertips and scatter them thinly across the top of the compost. (Pick a calm day to do this!)

**3** The seeds need to be covered with fine compost to help them grow. To do this, place a handful of compost in an old sieve or colander and shake it over the pot to break up any lumps. Keep doing this until you have a layer 1.5 cm thick. Write the name of the plant on a label and push it into the pot.

**4** Water the pot well, using a sprinkler head so that the water comes out gently and evenly. Put the pot in a sunny or slightly shaded spot.

## Looking after mixed salad leaves

- Keep the pot slightly moist until the seedlings start to grow, then water more to stop the compost from drying out.
- The plants will not grow very big if they are squashed together. Remove a few seedlings to leave about a 5 cm gap between plants.
- A pot of leaves will last for many weeks, but once they start to flower, they will taste bitter, so put any flowering plants in the compost.

### KATY SAYS
Sow a new pot every three weeks or whenever the pot is half empty, to make sure you always have leaves to pick.

**When to pick** You can pick leaves about three weeks after sowing. Snip off baby leaves from around the outside of plants with a pair of scissors (leave the centre, as this is where new leaves will grow from). (Remember, 'when using scissors everyone knows, it's best to point them at your toes'!)

# Grow your own lunchbox

An old plastic lunchbox makes a fun place to grow bite-sized vegetables and fruit. Sow or plant your favourites, put the lunchbox in a sunny spot and you'll soon be picking your own yummy lunch.

## When to do this

Spring    Summer

**1** Open your box up so you have two parts. Each part will need five or six holes in the bottom to allow water to drip out. Use a felt tip pen to mark where you want the holes to be, making sure they are not too close together. Ask an adult to make the holes with a bradawl or drill.

## What you will need:

- plastic lunchbox
- felt tip pen
- bradawl or drill
- multipurpose compost
- pencil
- packets of seeds, such as short-rooted radish, round-rooted carrots, mixed salad leaves or Little Gem lettuce
- plant labels
- trowel
- plants, such as dwarf tomato, Alpine strawberry, chilli peppers or patio sweet pepper
- watering can with rose head sprinkler

**2** Fill both sides of the lunchbox with compost, tickling any big lumps with your fingers to break them up and make the compost nice and smooth. Press down with your fingertips, leaving a small gap between the surface and the top of the box.

**3** In one side of the lunchbox, use a pencil to make short grooves in the compost. Try to make these as straight as possible and not too close together. Sow your seeds and cover them carefully with compost. Write the name of each plant on a label and push it into the compost at the start of each row.

**4** The other side of the lunchbox is for plants, but there will be room for only one large plant or two smaller ones. Dig however many holes you need with a trowel and put the plant(s) in place. Pour compost around the roots, push down and flatten the top with your fingers.

**5** Label each plant, then water the lunchbox using a watering can with a sprinkler to spread the water evenly. Put the box in a sunny place.

**KATY SAYS**

If you don't have a lunchbox, you could use an old plastic washing-up bowl instead.

### Looking after your pot

• Water the lunchbox often, especially during hot, dry weather.

• Put the lunchbox on a table, chair or bench to make it harder for slugs and snails to find.

• After picking your lovely lunchbox goodies, sow some more seeds or fill the gaps that are left by popping in other plants.

# Quick courgettes

You can grow your own courgette plants from seed or buy ready-grown plants. A single plant will produce loads of courgettes over the summer if you give it a sunny spot and lots of water. Courgettes belong to the same family of plants as melon, cucumbers and pumpkins.

**Plant**
June

**Flowers appear**
June to September

**Courgettes ready**
June to October

## What you will need:

- 30 cm pot
- multipurpose compost
- trowel
- courgette plant (bought or raised from your own seeds)
- plant label and pencil
- watering can with rose head sprinkler

**1** Fill your flowerpot with compost, tickling any big lumps with your fingers to break them up and make the compost nice and smooth. Press down with your fingertips, so that there is a 5 cm gap between the compost and the top of the pot.

**2** Dig a small hole in the centre of the pot with a trowel, making sure that it is the same size as the pot holding your courgette plant.

### KATY SAYS
You can eat courgette flowers either raw as part of a (very pretty) salad or stuffed with a filling and cooked. Delicious!

**3** Slide the plant out of its pot. Be careful not to break the roots, as the plant uses these for "drinking" when it is growing. Now place your plant gently in the hole. Pour more compost around the roots, then press down to keep the plant standing up straight.

**4** Press the top of the compost with your hand so it is nice and smooth. Write the name of the courgette plant on a label and stick it in the pot. This helps you to remember which plant is which.

**5** Water the pot well, using a sprinkler head so that the water comes out gently and evenly. Put the pot in the sunniest spot possible.

## Looking after courgettes

- Water courgette plants every day to keep the compost damp. Try not to overdo it, though, as plants in soggy compost will rot.
- You'll get more courgettes if you feed plants every week when they start flowering. Ask an adult to add a few drops of liquid tomato food to your watering can.
- The plants will provide you with courgettes from early summer to the middle of autumn. Pick them often to let new ones grow.

## When to pick
Courgettes are best picked when they are about 10 cm long. If you leave them on the plant for much longer, they will swell up like marrows and may lose their flavour. Ask an adult to remove them with sharp scissors, cutting through the tough stalk that holds them to the plant.

You can use your courgettes in Green Parcel Pie (page 74).

# Crunchy carrots

Nothing beats munching on your own sweet carrots. These bite-sized roots are tasty and juicy and really easy to grow. They are great in pots, hanging baskets or window boxes, but you could also try growing them in a sunny patch of soil.

**Sow seeds**
March to June

**Leaves appear**
April to September

**Carrots ready**
June to September

## What you will need:

- 20 cm pot
- soil-based compost (e.g. John Innes No. 3)
- packet of carrot seeds
- old colander or sieve
- plant label and pencil
- watering can with rose head sprinkler

**1** Fill your flowerpot with compost, tickling any big lumps with your fingers to break them up and make the compost nice and smooth. Press down with your fingertips, so that there is a 5 cm gap between the compost and the top of the pot.

### KATY SAYS
Short, round-rooted or baby carrots are best in pots. Other carrots can be grown in the ground. Dig the ground and remove any large stones, then sow the seeds, 1 cm deep, in short rows.

**2** Carefully tear off a corner of the seed packet and shake a few seeds into the palm of your hand. Pinch a few seeds with your fingertips and scatter them thinly across the surface of the compost, leaving a 3 cm gap between seeds.

**3** The seeds need to be covered with fine compost to help them grow. To do this, place a handful of compost in an old sieve or colander and shake it over the pot to break up any lumps. Keep doing this until you have a layer 1.5 cm thick. Write the name of the plant on a label and push it into the pot.

**DID YOU KNOW:**

Carrots are good for your eyes and skin.

**4** Water the pot well, using a sprinkler head so that the water comes out gently and evenly. Put the pot in the sunniest spot possible.

## Looking after carrots
• Keep plants well watered, especially during hot, sunny weather. If the compost is allowed to dry out, the roots may split apart, giving you funny fork-tailed carrots!

## When to pick
Most carrots will be ready for picking three months after sowing. Water the pots before pulling the carrots out, otherwise the roots may snap off. Only pick what you need to eat, then water again when you've finished to settle the compost around the other carrots.

You can use your carrots in Crunchy Coleslaw (page 64) and Sunny Carrot Cake (page 90).

# Hot potatoes

Plant some potatoes in a pot, keep it well watered and you'll soon be digging up lots of your own potatoes. Easy.

| **Chitting** | **Plant** | **Leaves appear** | **Flowers appear** | **Potatoes ready** |
| --- | --- | --- | --- | --- |
| February to April | March to May | March | June | June to July |

## What you will need:

- plastic bucket, 30 cm wide by 30 cm deep
- drill
- multipurpose compost
- two 'chitted' seed potatoes
- plant label and pencil
- watering can with rose head sprinkler

## 'Chitting' potatoes

Place two seed potatoes in the hollows of an egg carton and leave in a cool, light spot (indoors) for up to six weeks until they have formed little shoots, about 3 cm tall. This is called "chitting".

**DID YOU KNOW:**

Seed potatoes are small potatoes, rather than real seeds.

**1** Before planting, you need to prepare your bucket. Ask an adult to drill a few drainage holes in the base to allow water to escape.

**2** Spread a 15 cm layer of compost in the base of your bucket, tickling any large lumps with your fingers to break them up.

**3** Place your chitted potatoes carefully on the compost, with the delicate shoots facing upwards, taking care not to snap any of them. Cover with another 15 cm of compost. Write the name of the plant on a label and push it into the pot.

**4** Water the pot well, using a sprinkler head so that the water comes out gently and evenly. Put the pot in a sunny spot.

**5** When the leafy stems of the potatoes are about 20 cm tall, pour more compost into the pot, leaving just the tips of the plants showing.

**6** Keep adding more compost as the stems grow, until you are left with just a 5 cm gap between the surface of the compost and the top of the pot.

**KATY SAYS**

Potatoes come in many different colours, shapes and sizes – but small 'salad' potatoes are great in pots.

### Looking after potatoes
• Make sure the bucket is watered regularly so that the compost is never allowed to dry out.
• Feed plants weekly with a special potato fertiliser or a liquid seaweed fertiliser. Ask an adult to sprinkle the food on the compost or to add a few drops of a liquid fertiliser to your watering can.

**When to pick** Salad potatoes are ready for harvesting in summer when the plants are in full flower. Tip the bucket on its side and slightly loosen the compost by wriggling your fingers in it. Now comes the fun bit: comb your hands through the compost to fish out all the lovely new potatoes.

You can serve your salad potatoes with Herby Butter (page 62).

# Fun ideas in the garden

Here are some great ideas for other ways to have fun in the garden.

**Fun pots** You don't have to grow plants in normal pots. As long as there's room for some compost and space for the roots to grow, you can try using lots of items you might have in the house to make your garden really fun. An old tea pot, bright plastic cups, a colander, plastic jars are all perfect. Don't forget to ask if you can use the items before filling them with compost, or you could be unpopular... Get planting!

**Wildlife hunt** Go on a back garden safari. Spend a few minutes looking around your garden to see how many different creatures you can find. Look under stones, hedges, beneath leaves and in other nooks and crannies. Take along a magnifying glass to help spot really small bugs, and a pencil and piece of paper so you can draw a picture of the incredible creatures you see.

**KATY SAYS**

Why not try growing plants in an old pair of Wellington boots?

## Sunny sunflower race

It's great fun to have a competition to see who can grow the tallest sunflower. Ask an adult to invite your friends over and give everyone a pot, some sunflower seeds and some compost. Sow seeds 2.5 cm deep, water them and then take them home, putting them on a light window ledge indoors to germinate. The sunflowers can be planted in large pots or in soil outdoors in late spring. Measure the height of plants when they are in flower in late summer. The one with the tallest plant wins.

## Keep a garden diary

Write down the names of plants you grow and draw pictures of the amazing wildlife you see in the garden.

## Smelly plants

Squeeze or rub the leaves of these plants, then breathe in deeply to smell their lovely fragrance:

- Basil
- Chives
- Coriander
- Mint
- Rosemary
- Parsley
- Oregano
- Sage

## Potato prints

Potatoes are great to eat, but they can also be used to make fantastic pictures. Ask an adult to cut a raw potato in half, then dab the cut surfaces on a piece of kitchen towel to soak up the moisture. Draw a pattern, shape or even your name on the cut side with a felt tip pen, then ask an adult to cut around the shape with a knife to leave a raised section. Cover the potato shape in paint, then press onto your piece of white paper. Wipe the potato with kitchen towel to remove old paint before adding a new colour.

**What you will need**
- potato
- paper towel
- felt tip pen
- knife
- coloured paint and brushes
- piece of white paper

# Cool mint

Mint is an easy-to-grow herb that smells and tastes great. The stems die in autumn, but will grow again the following spring. Mini-beasts love mint flowers, so look out for them when you are picking some mint.

**Plant**
March to June

**Pick leaves**
May to early November

## What you will need:

- 30 cm pot
- soil-based compost (e.g. John Innes No. 3) mixed with an equal amount of multipurpose compost
- trowel
- mint plant
- plant label and pencil
- watering can with rose head sprinkler

**1** Fill your flowerpot with compost, tickling any big lumps with your fingers to break them up and make the compost nice and smooth. Shake it level, so that there is a 5 cm gap between the compost and the top of the pot.

**2** Dig a hole in the centre of the pot with a trowel: it needs to be the same size as the little pot holding your mint plant.

**3** Slide the plant out of its pot. Be careful with the roots. Now place your plant gently in the hole. Pour more compost around the roots, then press down to keep the plant standing up straight.

**4** Press the top of the compost with your hand so it is nice and smooth. Write the name of the mint plant on a label and stick it in the pot. This helps you to remember which plant is which.

**5** Water the pot well, using a sprinkler head so that the water comes out gently and evenly. Put the pot in the sunniest spot possible.

## Looking after mint

- Water plants regularly, especially during hot, dry weather. Remove the sprinkler from a watering can and pour directly onto the compost.
- Keep pots of different mint varieties spaced out so they keep their special scent and flavour.
- When plants have finished flowering, use scissors to chop the stems back to 5 cm, which will help new stems to grow.

You can use your mint in Cheesy Pasta Rolls (page 52) and Melon and Feta Salad (page 70).

**When to pick** You can start picking mint in spring, when the tips grow above the ground, and carry on until the stems die in autumn. You can pick leaves one at a time or pinch off whole shoots.

# Savoury thyme

This sun-loving herb has spicy-scented, strongly flavoured, evergreen leaves, so you can pick them all year round. There are nearly 200 different varieties, including plants with bright golden leaves.

**Plant**
mid-March to mid-May

**Pick leaves**
all year round

**DID YOU KNOW:**
Thyme is covered in pretty flowers over the summer that will attract insects such as bees.

## What you will need:

- 15 cm pot
- soil-based compost (e.g. John Innes No. 3)
- trowel
- thyme plant
- plant label and pencil
- watering can with rose head sprinkler

**1** Fill your flowerpot with compost, tickling any big lumps with your fingers to break them up and make the compost nice and smooth. Shake it level, so that there is a 5 cm gap between the compost and the top of the pot.

**2** Dig a hole in the centre of the pot with a trowel: it needs to be the same size as the little pot holding your thyme plant.

**3** Slide the plant out of its pot carefully. Now place your plant gently in the hole. Pour more compost around the roots, then press down to keep the plant standing up straight.

**4** Press the top of the compost with your hands so it is nice and smooth.

**5** Write the name of the thyme plant on a plant label and stick it in the pot.

**6** Water the pot well, using a sprinkler head so that the water comes out gently and evenly. Put the pot in the sunniest place possible.

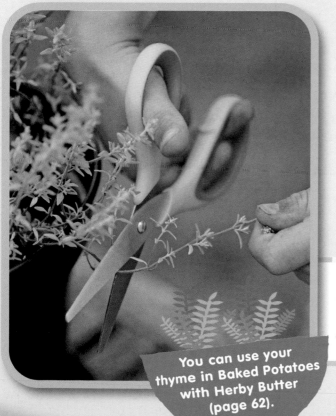

## Looking after thyme
• Thyme does not like too much water, so wait until the compost is dry before adding more.
• Thyme looks messy after it has finished flowering. Use scissors to give plants a 'hair cut' to make them look tidy.
• Thyme can be left outside in winter. Place the pot on large stones to let water trickle out of the holes in the bottom.

**When to pick** Snip off small shoots with scissors. (Remember, 'when using scissors, everyone knows, it's best to point them at your toes!').

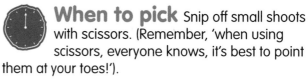
You can use your thyme in Baked Potatoes with Herby Butter (page 62).

# Edible wildlife garden

Mini-beasts are good for the garden. If you grow vegetables, herbs and fruit with nectar-rich flowers in a window box, you will get lots of lovely food to eat and attract the mini-beasts at same time. Win, win!

## When to do this

Spring    Summer

### KATY SAYS

Look out for butterflies, bees, ladybirds, hoverflies and other helpful creatures.

## What you will need:

- clay window box
- emulsion paint in white, red and black
- pebbles or bits of broken pot
- multipurpose compost
- selection of wildlife-friendly plants
- trowel
- gravel
- watering can with rose head sprinkler

**1** Make your wildlife garden really pretty by painting the window box with ladybird spots. First paint it with white undercoat, next paint it bright red and then add a few black spots. Let each coat of paint dry before adding another.

**2** Cover the bottom of the window box with a layer of pebbles or bits of broken clay pot. This will stop the drainage holes in the bottom from getting blocked up with compost.

**3** Fill up the window box with compost, tickling any big lumps with your fingers to break them up and make the compost smooth. Press down the compost your fingertips, then level with your hands, leaving a 5 cm gap between the surface and the top of the pot.

**4** Plan where you are going to put your plants by arranging them on the compost where you think they will look good. Upright plants are best in the middle or back, while trailing plants should be put at the front.

**5** Dig out small holes with a trowel and plant your vegetables, fruit and herbs. Fill any gaps around them with more compost.

**6** Cover the surface of the compost with gravel. This makes hiding places for mini-beasts and will stop weeds from growing.

## Looking after your window box
• Water your window box regularly, especially during hot, dry weather. Your plants won't be happy if the compost gets dry.
• When you have finished picking annual plants (ones that die at the end of the season), dig them out and put them on the compost heap. Fill the gaps with new plants in the spring.

Before cooking, wash your hands and put an apron on

# i can c🔵ok

# Lunch

# Scrunchy crunchy chicken

Serve the chicken with steamed carrots.

## Ingredients:

- 1 small cooked chicken breast (about 100–150 g weight)
- 1 rasher cooked bacon
- 3–4 button mushrooms
- 30–40 g (about 8) fine green beans
- 1 teaspoon chopped fresh tarragon leaves
- ½ cup single cream
- ½ teaspoon stock powder
- 2 teaspoons plain flour
- 20 g butter
- 2 large sheets filo pastry cut into 8 squares

## Equipment:

- workmat
- scales
- measuring jug
- 2 teaspoons
- scissors
- ovenproof dish (about 400ml capacity)
- 2 cups
- fork
- pastry brush
- baking tray
- oven gloves (for adult use)

**Serves 2**

## What to do

1 Weigh or measure all the ingredients. Cut the cooked chicken breast and the bacon up using the scissors and put into the bottom of the ovenproof dish. Break up the mushrooms and put on top.

### KATY SAYS

Brushing filo pastry with melted butter makes it lovely and crisp when it is cooked.

**2** Top and tail (remove the stalks and tails using fingers or scissors) the green beans, then snap into smaller lengths (about 2 cm) and add them to the dish.

**3** Put the fresh tarragon into a cup. Add the cream, then the stock powder. Stir in the flour with the fork, then pour all this over the meat mixture.

**4** Melt the butter in the other cup. You'll need to find an adult to help with this part. Lastly, brush the squares of filo pastry one at a time with melted butter and scrunch into rosettes and put these on top of your pie.

**5** Place the casserole dish on a baking tray.

**6** You'll need to ask an adult for help with this part. Put it in a preheated oven, 180°C fan, 200°C, Gas Mark 6, for 25–30 minutes or until the filo topping is golden and crispy and the filling is piping hot.

**Once the Scrunchy Crunchy Chicken has cooled down a little, you can eat it!**

# Cheesy pasta rolls

Serve the pasta with a green salad.

## Ingredients:

- vegetable oil for greasing
- ½ cup tinned chopped tomatoes
- pinch dried chilli flakes
- 100 g ricotta cheese
- 5 g fresh mint (a small handful)
- 10 g baby leaf spinach (a large handful)
- 1 fresh lasagne sheet (17 x 22 cm)
- 15 g ready-grated Cheddar cheese
- pinch of pepper

## Equipment:

- workmat
- scales
- 2 cups
- 2 forks
- mixing bowl
- scissors
- table knife
- ovenproof dish (about 400ml capacity) with a lid
- pastry brush
- baking tray
- oven gloves (for adult use)

**Serves 2**

### What to do

**1** Weigh or measure all the ingredients. Using the pastry brush, brush the ovenproof dish with oil.

**2** Put the tomatoes into one of the cups and add the chilli flakes. Stir with a fork, then pour enough of the mixture to cover the bottom of the cooking dish.

**KATY SAYS**

Make sure you completely cover the pasta rolls with the tomatoes.

**3** Put the ricotta and pepper into a bowl and mix with the other fork. Put the mint and spinach in the other cup and, using the scissors, cut them into smaller pieces. Add to the cheese in the bowl.

**4** Fold the lasagne sheet in half, matching the short sides. Gently run your fingers over the fold to help the pasta break in to two pieces.

**5** Spread the cheese mixture on the top of both pieces of lasagne, then roll them up into tubes, starting at a narrow edge.

**6** Place the rolled-up lasagne tubes in the dish on top of the layer of tomatoes. Now cover with the rest of the chopped tomatoes. Top with a sprinkling of grated cheese. Put the lid on and put the dish on the baking tray. You'll need to ask an adult for help with this part. Put it in a preheated oven, 200°C fan, 210°C, Gas Mark 7, for 15–20 minutes.

Once the Cheesy Pasta Rolls have cooled down a bit, you can eat them!

# Turkey snaps

Serve with seasonal vegetables and tomato sauce or chutney.

## Ingredients:

- vegetable oil for greasing
- 150 g fresh turkey mince
- 10 g fresh tarragon (a small handful)
- 1 egg
- 25 g plain flour
- 25 g puffed rice cereal
- pinch of pepper

## Equipment:

- workmat
- scales
- pastry brush
- baking tray and paper
- mixing bowl
- cup
- scissors
- fork
- dessertspoon
- 3 small bowls
- oven gloves (for adult use)

**Serves 2**

**What to do**

**1** Weigh or measure all the ingredients. Line the baking tray with baking paper and brush it with oil, using the pastry brush.

**2** Put the mince into the mixing bowl. Add a pinch of pepper. Using your fingers, pull the leaves off the tarragon and put these into the cup. Chop them up with the scissors then add these too. Mix with the fork.

**3** Break the egg into the cup and beat it. Add a little of the egg (about a dessertspoon) to the mince to help it 'bind' (stick together). Stir well with the fork again.

**4** Put the flour in a small bowl, the leftover beaten egg in another small bowl and the puffed rice into the third small bowl and arrange them in front of you.

**5** Divide the mince mixture into 4 even sized portions by making a line through the middle of the mixture in the bowl to make 2 portions, then turn the bowl and do this again – making 4 portions.

**Once the Turkey Snaps have cooled down a little, you can eat them!**

**6** Shape the first portion of the mince by squashing the mixture quite firmly in the palm of your hand to make a ball or burger shape. Then roll the shaped mince in the flour in the first bowl. Then roll it all over in the egg. Then roll it in the puffed rice. Now place it on the baking tray and start the process again until you have made 4. Lightly dab the top of the Turkey Puffs with some oil.

**7** You'll need to ask an adult for help with this part. Put the baking tray in the centre of a preheated oven, 180°C fan, 200°C, Gas Mark 6, for around 15 minutes or until cooked through.

**Turkey snaps 55**

# Chicken in a basket

Serve the chicken with
a green salad.

## Ingredients:

- vegetable oil for greasing
- 1 medium slice bread
- 1 dessertspoon plain yogurt
- 1 dessertspoon mayonnaise
- ½ teaspoon korma curry paste
- 1 dessertspoon mango chutney
- around 50 g cooked chicken
- 1 tablespoon grapes

## Equipment:

- workmat
- scales
- 3 dessertspoons
- teaspoon
- tablespoon
- individual tin, e.g. quiche tin, about 10 cm in diameter or similar
- pastry brush
- baking tray
- rolling pin
- table knife
- mixing bowl
- oven gloves (for adult use)

**What to do**

**Serves 1**

**1** Weigh or measure all the ingredients. Oil the inside of the quiche tin, using a pastry brush. Place it on a baking tray.

**2** First roll out the slice of bread so that it is really flat. Cut off the crusts with the table knife and line the tin with the bread. Gently dab the top of the bread with oil.

**3** You'll need to ask an adult for help with this part. Put it in a preheated oven, 170°C fan, 190°C, Gas Mark 5, for 10 minutes to crisp up.

**4** While the bread basket is cooking, put the yogurt and mayonnaise into the mixing bowl. Add the curry paste and chutney, and stir. Tear up the cooked chicken and add to the bowl.

**5** Halve the grapes, using the table knife, or tear apart. Put two pieces of grape on one side and add the rest to the bowl. Mix all the ingredients together.

**6** Remove the bread basket from the oven and allow to cool. Put the chicken filling in, top with the reserved fresh grape pieces and chill for about 30 minutes and then eat it.

**KATY SAYS**

Add a little extra curry paste if you want it to taste more spicy.

Once the Chicken in a Basket has been chilled for a bit, you can eat it!

# Seaside bites

Serve these fish bites with tomatoes.

## Ingredients:

- vegetable oil for greasing
- 2 medium slices bread
- 1 egg
- 1 tablespoon milk
- 40 g fresh trout fillet (skinned and boned)
- fresh chives
- ½ teaspoon mild horseradish
- pinch of pepper

## Equipment:

- workmat
- tablespoon
- scales
- teaspoon
- 2 cupcake moulds
- pastry brush
- rolling pin
- 8–9 cm cutter
- mixing bowl
- fork
- scissors
- cup
- baking tray
- oven gloves (for adult use)

**Serves 2**

## What to do

**1** Weigh or measure all the ingredients. Start by liberally oiling the inside of two large cupcake moulds with vegetable oil and the pastry brush.

**2** Now roll the 2 slices of bread flat with the rolling pin, pressing down well, then use the cutter to cut 2 circles.

**3** Break the egg into the mixing bowl, add a pinch of pepper and the milk and whisk up with the fork. Dip the circles of bread into the eggy mixture then push the circles into the prepared cupcake moulds.

**KATY SAYS**

Press hard on the rolling pin to squash the bread flat.

**4** Take the fillet and cut into bite-sized pieces with scissors and add them to leftover egg mixture.

**5** Put the chives into the bottom of the cup and chop with the scissors. Add to the eggy mix along with the horseradish.

**6** Put the moulds on the baking tray. Pour the remaining eggy mixture into the eggy-bread-lined cases. You may not get it all in.

**7** You'll need to ask an adult for help with this part. Place in a preheated oven, 180°C fan, 200°C, Gas Mark 6, for 20–25 minutes or until golden and set.

**Once the Seaside Bites have cooled down a little, you can eat them!**

# Haddock puff

Serve this fish pie with some carrot batons and cherry tomatoes.

## Ingredients:

- 50 g fresh skinless boneless smoked haddock
- 1 tablespoon crème fraîche
- 10 g watercress (about a handful)
- 125 g (¼ block) puff pastry
- pinch of pepper

## Equipment:

- workmat
- scales
- tablespoon
- baking tray and paper
- scissors
- mixing bowl
- tea towel
- fork
- flour dredger
- rolling pin
- pastry brush
- table knife
- oven gloves (for adult use)

**What to do**

**Serves 2**

**1** Weigh or measure all the ingredients. Line the baking tray with baking paper.

**2** Start by cutting up the haddock into bite sized pieces with scissors. Put the fish in to a mixing bowl and then add the crème fraîche. Add some pepper.

**KATY SAYS**

Look and feel for any bones when you are cutting up the fish and carefully take them out.

**3** Wash the watercress and dry off as much as possible on a tea towel. Pinch and pull the leaves off the stalks and put in the mixing bowl with the crème fraîche and fish. Stir with the fork and put the bowl to one side.

**4** Roll out the pastry into a rectangle, (don't forget to use the dredger to flour the surface first), to about 5 mm thick and about A5 in size.

**5** With the pastry positioned with the short edge closest to you, place the fish mixture on to the bottom half of the rectangle, leaving 1 cm border around the edges. Add a little water to the used mixing bowl and use this and the pastry brush to brush the edges of the pastry. This will help them stick together.

**6** Bring the top half of the pastry down to cover the mixture to seal in the fish mixture, like an envelope. Fold and press the edges together firmly with your fingers. Trim the edges with the knife and make a small slit in the top with the table knife to let the steam out.

**7** Now brush the top of the parcel with the remaining water from the mixing bowl – this makes a glaze. Put the parcel on the baking tray.

**8** You'll need to ask an adult for help with this part. Put in a preheated oven, 210°C fan, 220°C, Gas Mark 7, for 25–30 minutes or until golden brown.

Once the Haddock Puff has cooled down a little, you can eat it!

# Baked potatoes with herby butter

Serve the potatoes with some green vegetables or cooked meat.

## Ingredients:

- 4 small/medium baking potatoes
- vegetable oil for coating the potatoes
- few leaves of herbs; such as parsley, chives, basil, mint, thyme, tarragon, sage (total weight about 20 g)
- 1 garlic clove (optional)
- 75 g soft unsalted butter
- pinch of pepper

## Equipment:

- workmat
- scales
- scrubbing brush or cloth
- kitchen paper or clean tea towel
- fork
- cup
- scissors
- small mixing bowl
- plastic bag
- rolling pin
- baking paper cut to fit serving dish
- small serving dish for butter
- oven gloves (for adult use)

**Serves 4**

## What to do

**1** Weigh or measure all the ingredients. Wash and scrub the potatoes in water – rinse them well to make sure you have all the earth off them. Pat them dry with kitchen paper or a clean tea towel.

**2** Prick with the fork to make holes to let the steam escape then put some oil on your hands and rub the skins with oil.

**3** You'll need to ask an adult for help with this part. Put the potatoes straight on to the oven shelves in a preheated oven, 180°C fan, 200°C, Gas Mark 6, for about 1–1½ hours.

**4** While the potatoes are cooking, make the herb butter. Break the leaves off each of the herbs in turn, put them all together in the cup and chop with scissors.

**5** If using garlic, remove the papery skin and then put into the plastic bag and bash with the rolling pin. Then put the garlic in the mixing bowl with the herbs. Dispose of the plastic bag carefully.

**KATY SAYS**

The herby butter can be kept in the fridge for a few days with its paper lid on.

**6** Add the soft butter and the pepper to the mixing bowl with the garlic and herbs. Now mash the mixture with the fork. To get the mixture started use the back of the fork to do the mashing and then mix as usual. Put into the serving dish.

Ask a grown up to split the baked potatoes and then add some of your tasty butter

# Crunchy coleslaw

Serve this coleslaw with cooked meats or a baked potato.

## Ingredients:

- 1 small dessert apple
- 1 medium carrot
- ½ a small white cabbage, cut in half
- 2 dessertspoons mayonnaise
- 1 dessertspoon raisins
- pinch of pepper

## Equipment:

- workmat
- dessertspoon
- grater
- mixing bowl

**Serves 4**

## What to do

**1** Weigh or measure all the ingredients. Wash the apple and carrot (there is no need to peel them). You will need to ask an adult to core the apple for you and halve and then quarter the cabbage.

**2** First, grate the cabbage using the largest holes on the grater and put the gratings in the mixing bowl.

**3** Next, snap the carrot in half, grate it and add to the bowl. Grate the apple and add this to the bowl.

**4** Now stir all three ingredients together with the mayonnaise. Add the raisins and the pepper to finish. Store covered in the fridge until ready to eat it.

### KATY SAYS

Don't put in too much mayonnaise to start with. You can always add more, but you can't take it out!

**Once the Coleslaw has chilled in the fridge for a bit, you can eat it!**

# Treasure chest tart

Serve this vegetable tart with carrot batons.

## Ingredients:

- 4 cherry tomatoes
- 4 basil leaves
- pinch of paprika
- 1 spring onion
- 1 teaspoon olive oil
- ¼ fresh green pepper
- 1 dessertspoon tinned or fresh sweetcorn
- 125 g (¼ block) puff pastry

## Equipment:

- workmat
- scales
- teaspoon
- dessertspoon
- baking tray and paper
- cup
- scissors
- mixing bowl
- flour dredger
- rolling pin (optional)
- table knife
- oven gloves (for adult use)

**Serves 1**

## What to do

**1** Weigh or measure all the ingredients. Line the baking tray with baking paper.

**2** Count out the tomatoes into the cup, then snip them into pieces with the scissors – they may squirt, so be careful. Put them into the mixing bowl.

**3** Rip and tear the basil leaves and add them to the bowl with the paprika. Chop up the spring onion into small pieces with the scissors and add to the bowl. Stir in the olive oil.

**KATY SAYS**

Put the pastry on to the baking tray before adding the topping, as it will be too difficult to move afterwards.

**4** Pop open the pepper and tear about a quarter of it into bite-sized pieces. Add this to the other ingredients with the sweetcorn.

**5** Now dust the surface of the pastry with the dredger and either roll it out or pat it flat with your fist.

**6** Trim to an even shape with the knife and mark a border, like a picture frame, by not cutting through the pastry completely.

**7** Put the pastry onto the paper-lined baking tray. Pile the vegetable filling into the central part of the pastry and spread it out to the edges of the inner rectangle using the knife.

**8** You'll need to ask an adult for help with this part. Put it in a preheated oven, 200°C fan, 220°C, Gas Mark 7, for 15–20 minutes until the pastry is golden and risen.

**Once the Treasure Chest Tart has cooled down a little, you can eat it!**

# Baked explorer pancakes

Serve the pancakes with pieces of fresh red and orange pepper.

## Ingredients:

- vegetable oil for greasing
- 1 egg
- 2 dessertspoons milk
- 2 spring onions
- 10 g fresh coriander (about a small handful)
- 2 dessertspoons sweetcorn
- 30–40 g (about 8) green beans
- 50 g plain flour
- ½ teaspoon baking powder
- pinch of pepper

## Equipment:

- workmat
- dessertspoon
- scales
- teaspoon
- pastry brush
- baking tray and paper
- 2 cups
- fork or whisk
- scissors
- 2 mixing bowls
- oven gloves (for adult use)

**Serves 2**

**What to do**

**1** Weigh or measure all the ingredients. Line the baking tray with baking paper and brush it with oil, using the pastry brush.

**2** Break the egg into a cup, add the milk and stir with a fork or whisk.

### KATY SAYS

Flatten the spoonfuls of batter with the back of the spoon for the best pancakes.

**3** Chop up the spring onions with the scissors, topping and tailing to take off the roots and the dark green part. Put into a mixing bowl. Put the fresh coriander in another cup and cut up using the scissors. Add the coriander to the mixing bowl then add the sweetcorn.

**4** Top and tail (remove the stalks and tails using fingers or scissors) the beans and cut them or snap them into small pieces (about 2 cm) – add to the mixing bowl. Stir all the ingredients together. Then add the eggy mixture to the vegetables.

**5** Prepare the flour and baking powder together in another bowl by stirring them together and then add to the vegetable mixture and stir with the fork or whisk to form a smooth batter. It will be quite thick. Add the pepper.

**6** Drop 4 heaped dessertspoons of the mixture on to the paper-lined baking tray to make 4 pancakes. Spread each flat with the spoon.

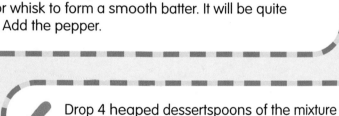

**7** You'll need to ask an adult for help with this part. Put it in a preheated oven, 200°C fan, 220°C, Gas Mark 7, for 10 minutes.

Once the Baked Explorer Pancakes have cooled down a little, you can eat them!

# Melon & feta salad with redcurrants

Serve the salad with some crusty bread.

## Ingredients:

- ½ fresh melon (any melon will do except a watermelon)
- 100 g feta cheese
- 10 g fresh mint (about a small handful)
- ½ lemon
- 1 tablespoon fresh redcurrants (approximate weight 25–30 g)
- pinch of pepper

## Equipment:

- workmat
- scales
- tablespoon
- cutting board
- sharp knife (for adult use)
- melon baller or teaspoon
- mixing bowl
- cup
- scissors
- large plate

**Serves 2-3**

## What to do

**1** Weigh or measure all the ingredients. Ask your adult to use the sharp knife to cut the melon and lemon in half on the cutting board.

**2** Scoop the seeds out of one half of the melon using the tablespoon. Then using the melon baller or a teaspoon, empty the flesh from the inside making balls or curls and put it into the mixing bowl. Drain off any remaining juice from the melon half – and save the juice to drink later.

**3** Using your hands crumble the feta up into bite-sized chunks and mix with the melon. Put the fresh mint leaves in the cup and using the scissors cut them up and add to the melon and cheese mix. Squeeze the juice of ½ lemon over the top and add a pinch of pepper. Finally, pinch off all the stalks from the redcurrants and stir them into your salad mix.

**4** Put the melon half on a large plate and then spoon the salad mixture you have made back into the empty half of the melon. Serve straight from the shell.

**KATY SAYS**

Melons are big and need a sharp knife so ask an adult to help you cut it in half.

**Once the Melon & Feta Salad with Redcurrants is ready, you can eat it!**

# Green parcel pie

Serve this pie with some cooked peppers.

## Ingredients:

- 50–60 g courgette
- 1 egg
- 100 g soft cream cheese with chives
- 1 tablespoon ready-grated Parmesan cheese
- 40–50 ml rapeseed oil
- 3 sheets filo pastry
- pinch of pepper

## Equipment:

- workmat
- scales
- tablespoon
- measuring jug
- grater
- 2 mixing bowls
- fork
- pastry brush
- small loaf tin (500 g size)
- baking tray
- oven gloves (for adult use)

Serves 2

## What to do

**1** Weigh or measure all the ingredients. Start by making the pie filling. Grate the courgette into a bowl and put to one side ready for later.

**2** Break the egg into the other bowl, then beat it up with the fork. Then add the cream cheese and mix into the egg using the fork. Add the Parmesan and some pepper. Stir well, then add the grated courgette and give the mixture another good stir.

**KATY SAYS**

The overlaps of pastry become the lid of the pie.

**3** Brush the inside of the loaf tin with the oil and line with a sheet of filo pastry allowing the extra to fall over the outside of the tin. Dot with more oil then lay another sheet on top, creating extra overlap on the side. Add the third sheet on top.

**4** Pour your cheesy filling into the pie then fold the leftover pastry over the top, a layer at a time, hiding the filling. Dot the pastry with oil as you build the layers. Lastly dot the top of filo pastry with more oil.

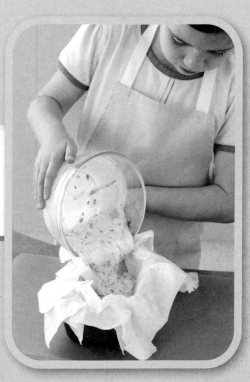

**5** You'll need to ask an adult for help with this part. Put the tin on a baking tray and then put in a preheated oven at 180°C fan, 200°C, Gas Mark 6, for 20–25 minutes or until the filo topping is golden and crispy.

**Once the Green Parcel Pie has cooled down a little, you can eat it!**

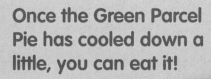

# Pepper boats

Serve these stuffed peppers with some crusty French bread.

## Ingredients:

- 1 red or orange pepper
- 4 cherry tomatoes
- 1 tablespoon olive oil
- 1 dessertspoon pine nuts
- 4 basil leaves
- 30 g soft goats' cheese
- pinch of pepper

## Equipment:

- workmat
- tablespoon
- dessertspoon
- scales
- mixing bowl
- scissors
- baking tray
- oven gloves (for adult use)

**What to do**

**Serves 2**

**1** Weigh or measure all the ingredients. Pop the pepper by pushing down on the stalk with your thumbs until you push it inside – then tear the pepper carefully to make two even-sized halves. These are your boats. Knock the pepper halves upside down to shake out all the seeds.

**2** Count the tomatoes into the bowl then chop them up with the scissors. Add the oil and a pinch of pepper and stir well.

**3** Now add in the pine nuts and finally tear up the basil leaves and add these too. Give the mixture a good stir with the tablespoon.

**4** Divide the mixture in two down the middle of the bowl using the tablespoon, then spoon the filling into the pepper boats.

**KATY SAYS**

Goats' cheese is very crumbly, so you can just break it up with your fingers.

**5** Finally, crumble the goat's cheese on top of the tomato mixture. Put the boats on the baking tray.

**6** You'll need to ask an adult for help with this part. Put it in a preheated oven, 180°C fan, 200°C, Gas Mark 6, for 20–25 minutes or until the cheese topping is golden.

Once the Pepper Boats have cooled down a little, you can eat them!

Before cooking, wash your hands and put an apron on

# i can cook
# Tea

# Chunky cheese loaf

**Serve this bread with extra slices of fresh apple.**

## Ingredients:

- vegetable oil for greasing
- 160 g plain flour
- 1 teaspoon baking powder
- 20 g soft butter
- 80 g (1) fresh apple
- 60 g mature Cheddar cheese
- 1 egg
- up to 50 ml apple juice

## Equipment:

- workmat
- scales
- teaspoon
- measuring jug
- small loaf tin (500 g size)
- pastry brush
- baking tray
- mixing bowl
- table knife
- grater
- fork
- tablespoon
- spatula
- oven gloves (for adult use)

**Makes 5–6 slices**

**What to do**

**1** Weigh or measure all the ingredients. Grease the loaf tin with oil using the pastry brush and place it on the baking tray.

**2** Put the flour, baking powder and butter together in the mixing bowl. Rub them together with your fingers (as if you were tickling the mixture) until you get a fine crumbly mixture.

**3** Ask an adult to help you cut up the apple with the table knife into small bite-sized pieces. Put them flat side down so the pieces don't wobble while you cut them. Add these to the bowl.

**KATY SAYS**

Practise rubbing your mixture together by tickling your grown up.

**4** Grate the cheese using the large side of the grater so you get bigger pieces and add 40 g to the flour mix.

**5** Now break the egg in the measuring jug and beat it with the fork. Then add to the mixture. You may need to add some of the apple juice to moisten the mixture – it should feel and look like a thick cake mix.

**6** Spoon it into the loaf tin, using the spatula to scrape out all the mix, and sprinkle the top with the remaining 20 g grated cheese, pressing down with your hands so it sticks to the surface.

**7** You'll need to ask an adult for help with this part. Put in a preheated oven, 160°C fan, 180°C, Gas Mark 4, for 40–50 minutes, or until the loaf is golden brown and has risen well.

**Once the Chunky Cheese Loaf has cooled down, you can eat it!**

# Cheese and tomato melts

Serve these biscuits with slices of apple.

## Ingredients:

- 75 g plain flour
- large pinch of mild paprika
- 20 g soft butter
- 1 spring onion
- 20 g mature Cheddar cheese, grated
- 2–3 tablespoons tomato juice

## Equipment:

- workmat
- scales
- grater
- tablespoon
- baking tray and paper
- mixing bowl
- scissors
- fork
- flour dredger
- rolling pin
- biscuit cutter (5 cm diameter)
- oven gloves (for adult use)

Makes 6–8 depending on the cutter size

**What to do**

**1** Weigh or measure all the ingredients. Line the baking tray with baking paper.

**2** Put the flour, paprika and butter together in the mixing bowl. Rub them together with your fingers (as if you were tickling the mixture) until you get a fine crumbly mixture.

**3** Cut the spring onion up into small pieces with the scissors, take off the roots and the dark green leaves first (topping and tailing). Start by cutting it into chunks, then add to the bowl and chop more in the bowl.

**KATY SAYS**

If the mixture doesn't stick together well in step 4, add some more tomato juice until it becomes a smooth dough.

**4** Next, stir the grated cheese in with the fork. Add 2 tablespoons of the tomato juice and mix with the spoon. Mix well.

**5** Put onto a floured surface (use the dredger) and roll flat (about 1 cm) with the rolling pin, then cut with the biscuit cutter. Place the biscuits on the baking tray.

**6** You'll need to ask an adult for help with this part. Put in a preheated oven, 180°C fan, 200°C, Gas Mark 6, for 10–15 minutes or until firm.

Once the Cheese and Tomato Melts have cooled down a little, you can eat them!

# Mini cheese munchies

Serve one or two of these little savoury cakes with ham.

## Ingredients:

- vegetable oil for greasing
- 1 egg
- 1 tablespoon polenta (quick cook, dried)
- 1 cup young leaf spinach
- 100 g plain cottage cheese
- pinch of mild chilli powder
- 45 g plain flour
- ground black pepper

## Equipment:

- workmat
- tablespoon
- cup
- scales
- 6-hole mini muffin tray
- pastry brush
- baking tray
- fork
- mixing bowl
- scissors
- 2 dessertspoons
- spatula
- oven gloves (for adult use)

**Makes 6**

## What to do

**1** Weigh and measure all the ingredients. Brush the mini muffin tray with oil using the pastry brush. Stand the muffin tray on the baking tray.

**2** Break the egg into your cup and beat it with the fork, then add the polenta – this allows the polenta to soften slightly before cooking.

**3** Prepare the spinach by pulling off the long stalks, then put into the mixing bowl and snip into small pieces using the scissors.

**4** To the spinach add the cottage cheese, chilli powder and black pepper. Then stir in the egg and polenta mix with one of the dessertspoons. Sprinkle the plain flour over the mixture and stir again until there is no flour visible.

**5** Spoon the mixture into the muffin holes using the 2-spoon method. Use the spatula to get all the mixture out of the bowl.

**6** You'll need to ask an adult for help with this part. Put in a preheated oven, 180°C fan, 200°C, Gas Mark 6, for 12–15 minutes until brown on top. Leave to cool.

Once the Mini Cheese Munchies have cooled down a little, you can eat them!

# Playtime popovers

Serve one or two of these savoury muffins with a glass of fresh juice.

## Ingredients:

- vegetable oil for greasing
- 1 egg
- 50 g plain flour
- 100 ml milk
- ½ teaspoon wholegrain mustard
- 2 closed-cup or small mushrooms
- 1 rasher of cooked bacon
- 2 cherry tomatoes

## Equipment:

- workmat
- scales
- measuring jug
- teaspoon
- pastry brush
- large 6-hole muffin tray
- baking tray
- cup
- fork or whisk
- mixing bowl
- scissors
- oven gloves (for adult use)

**What to do**

**Makes 4**

**1** Weigh and measure all the ingredients. Brush the muffin tray with vegetable oil using the pastry brush and place it on a baking tray.

**2** Break the egg into your cup and beat it with the fork or whisk. Put the flour into the mixing bowl and add the egg and stir.

**KATY SAYS**

You may not need all the wet mixture, depending on the size of your baking container.

**3** Add the milk to the mixing bowl and stir again until you have lots of bubbles and all the flour disappears.

**4** Add the mustard. This mixture is called a batter. Pour the batter from the mixing bowl into the measuring jug that had the milk in it.

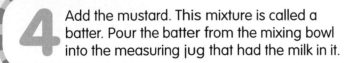

**5** Tear up the mushrooms and divide the pieces between the muffin cups. Using the scissors, cut up the bacon into small pieces and divide this up between the muffin cups too. Then chop the tomatoes in the cup that had the egg in and share equal amounts of this between the muffin cups. Finally, pour the batter over the top.

**6** You'll need to ask an adult for help with this part. Put it in a preheated oven, 200°C fan, 220°C, Gas Mark 7, for 15–20 minutes until brown on top. Leave to cool.

**Once the Playtime Popovers have cooled down a little, you can eat them!**

# Fig and fudge biscuits

Serve one or two of these biscuits with some red grapes or more dried figs.

## Ingredients:

- 60 g plain flour
- 40 g soft butter
- 1 ready-to-eat dried fig (20–25 g)
- 20 g caster sugar
- 1 tablespoon small fudge pieces

## Equipment:

- workmat
- scales
- tablespoon
- baking tray and paper
- mixing bowl
- scissors
- fork
- oven gloves (for adult use)

**Makes 8**

### What to do

**KATY SAYS**

Adding the sugar and fudge makes the mixture sweet.

**1** Weigh or measure all the ingredients. Line the baking tray with baking paper.

**2** Put the flour and butter into the mixing bowl and rub the two together to make a crumbly mixture – it is a bit like tickling the ingredients.

**3** Now snip the stalk off the dried fig then rip and snip the fruit into small pieces using the scissors. Add to the other ingredients.

**4** Add the sugar and the fudge pieces. Stir with the fork.

**5** Then use your hands to start to squeeze it all together; you can push down with your knuckles into the bowl. As it starts to make a lump, turn the bowl out onto the mat and continue squeezing to make a long, fat sausage shape.

**6** Tear the mixture in half – then pull each piece into half again then each smaller piece into 2, trying to keep them about the same size. This makes 8 pieces of biscuit dough.

**7** Roll each piece into a round ball then put onto the baking tray and flatten a little with your hand.

**8** You'll need to ask an adult for help with this part. Put in a preheated oven, 160°C fan, 180°C, Gas Mark 4, for 12–15 minutes or until lightly golden. Leave to cool on the paper.

Once the Fig and Fudge Biscuits have cooled down completely, you can eat them!

# Sunny carrot cake

Serve slices of this cake with some carrot sticks.

## Ingredients:

- 4 tablespoons vegetable oil, plus some for greasing
- 1 egg
- 60 g self-raising flour
- 60 g caster sugar
- 40 g carrot
- 30 g tinned crushed pineapple (drained)
- 20 g chopped walnuts (optional)

## Equipment:

- workmat
- tablespoon
- scales
- small loaf tin (500 g size)
- baking paper
- pastry brush
- 2 mixing bowls
- fork
- grater
- wooden spoon
- baking tray
- oven gloves (for adult use)

**Makes 6–8 slices**

## What to do

**1** Weigh or measure all the ingredients. Brush some oil inside the loaf tin. Line the base of the tin with some baking paper.

**2** Break the egg into a mixing bowl. Add the oil and whisk lightly with the fork.

### KATY SAYS

When whisking the wet ingredients, try to make as many bubbles as you can.

**3** Put the flour and sugar in to the other bowl. Stir with the fork. This is the 'dry' bowl.

**4** Grate the carrot and put it into the egg mixture. Next add the pineapple and walnuts. This is the 'wet' bowl.

**5** Pour the contents of the wet bowl into the dry bowl and mix well with the wooden spoon.

**6** Put the mixture into the loaf tin and place the loaf tin on a baking tray.

**7** You'll need to ask an adult for help with this part. Put in a preheated oven, 180°C fan, 200 °C, Gas Mark 5, 25–30 minutes. Leave to cool before tipping out and serving in slices.

Once the Sunny Carrot Cake has cooled down a little, you can eat it!

# Spiced fun buns

Serve these buns with some fresh fruit.

## Ingredients:

- 3 dessertspoons currants
- 1 dessertspoon chopped peel
- 2 dessertspoons caster sugar
- 110 g self-raising flour
- large pinch of mixed spice
- 60 g soft butter
- 1 egg (but you will not need all of it)

## Equipment:

- workmat
- dessertspoon
- scales
- baking tray and paper
- pastry brush
- 2 mixing bowls
- fork
- cup
- oven gloves (adult use)

Makes 8

## What to do

**1** Weigh or measure all the ingredients. Line the baking tray with baking paper and brush it with oil, using the pastry brush.

### KATY SAYS

Be careful to stir in the sugar, currants and peel gently.

**2** Put the currants, chopped peel and the sugar in one of the bowls.

**3** Put the flour, mixed spice and the butter in the other bowl. Rub in (tickle) the butter and flour and spice together until the mixture looks like fine breadcrumbs.

**4** Add the sugar, fruit and peel to the flour bowl and mix with the fork.

**5** Break the egg into the cup and beat with the fork, then add some (but not all) to your fruity mixture. The mixture should be firm enough to shape but not dry. Add a bit more egg if it is too dry to shape.

**6** Using your hands, tear the mixture in half, then in half again, then each piece in half until you have 8 pieces. Now, without shaping them (so leaving them rough), place them onto the baking tray.

**7** You'll need to ask an adult for help with this part. Put in a preheated oven, 180°C fan, 200°C, Gas Mark 6, for 15–20 minutes. Leave to cool on the baking tray.

Once the Spiced Fun Buns have cooled down a little, you can eat them!

# Picnic parkin

Serve the parkin with a glass of milk.

## Ingredients:

- 2 dessertspoons vegetable oil, plus some for greasing
- 50 g plain flour
- 1 teaspoon baking powder
- 1 tablespoon dark soft brown sugar
- ½ teaspoon ground ginger
- 40 g rolled oats
- 4 dessertspoons milk
- 5 dessertspoons golden syrup

## Equipment:

- workmat
- dessertspoon
- scales
- teaspoon
- tablespoon
- pastry brush
- small loaf tin (500 g size)
- 2 mixing bowls
- fork
- spatula
- baking tray
- oven gloves (adult use)

**Makes 5–8 slices**

## What to do

**1** Weigh or measure all the ingredients. Brush some oil inside the loaf tin.

**2** Put the flour in a mixing bowl with the baking powder, sugar and ginger. This is called the dry mixture.

**3** Put the oats and milk together in the other bowl and put to one side for 5–10 minutes so that the oats soak up the milk and soften up to help make a really chewy cake! Add the oil and then the golden syrup into the oats and milk. This is called the wet mixture.

**4** Pour the dry mixture into the wet mixture and stir with the fork until all the ingredients are well mixed. It should be a sloppy mixture.

**5** Pour the mixture into the prepared loaf tin, using the spatula to get all the mixture out of the bowl. Put the loaf tin on the baking tray

**6** You'll need to ask an adult for help with this part. Put in a preheated oven, 160°C fan, 180°C, Gas Mark 4, for 25–30 minutes or until risen and golden.

### KATY SAYS

If you measure the oil first, the golden syrup will slide off the spoon more easily.

**Once the Picnic Parkin has cooled down, you can eat it!**

# Spiced parsnip cake

Add the icing if you want an extra-special cake.

## Ingredients:

- 50 ml vegetable oil, plus some for greasing
- 50 g self-raising flour
- 50 g caster sugar
- 1 egg
- 50–60 g parsnip
- 1 teaspoon mixed spice
- 1 tablespoon pumpkin seeds or walnuts
- 40 g chopped dried apricots

For the icing:
- 20 g very soft butter
- 50 g cream cheese
- 2 teaspoons runny honey
- large pinch of mixed spice
- 1 tablespoon icing sugar.

## Equipment:

- workmat
- measuring jug
- scales
- teaspoon
- tablespoon
- small loaf tin (500 g size) or 4 large muffin cases
- pastry brush
- mixing bowl
- wooden spoon
- scrubbing brush
- grater
- baking tray
- oven gloves (for adult use)

**1 small cake or 4 large muffins**

## What to do

**1** Weigh or measure all the ingredients. Oil the inside of the loaf tin using the pastry brush.

**2** Put the flour, caster sugar and vegetable oil into the mixing bowl. Break the egg into the measuring jug. Add to the mixing bowl and stir with the wooden spoon to mix thoroughly.

**3** Scrub the parsnip, then grate and add this to the mixing bowl.

**4** Add the spice, seeds and the chopped apricots and give the mix a final stir. Pour the mix into the prepared loaf tin, or divide into 4 large muffins cases, and place on a baking tray.

**5** You'll need to ask an adult for help with this part. Place in a preheated oven, 180°C fan, 200°C, Gas Mark 6, for 25–30 minutes if using a loaf tin or 15–20 minutes if using 4 large muffin cases.

**6** The icing is optional. Once the cake has cooled, you can make the icing by mixing all the ingredients together really well in a bowl and spreading on the top.

**KATY SAYS**

Dried apricots are a colourful, tasty and healthy treat.

**Once the Spiced Parsnip Cake has cooled down a little, you can eat it!**

# Fruity filo parcels

Serve the parcels with plain yogurt.

## Ingredients:

- 1 tinned pear
- 4 teaspoons mixed dried fruit
- 30 g unsalted butter
- large pinch of mixed spice
- 1 teaspoon caster sugar
- 4 sheets filo pastry

## Equipment:

- workmat
- teaspoon
- scales
- baking tray and paper
- cup
- 2 mixing bowls
- scissors
- pastry brush
- oven gloves (for adult use)

**What to do**

**Serves 1–2**

**1** Weigh or measure all the ingredients. Line the baking tray with baking paper.

**2** Drain the pear and save the juice. Put the mixed dried fruit in the cup, add some pear juice from the tinned fruit and put to one side.

**3** Chop up the pear in one of the bowls with the scissors. Add the mixed fruit without any of the pear juice.

**4** Melt the butter in the other bowl (ask an adult to do this for you) and add the mixed spice and the sugar. Stir with the teaspoon. Spread out a sheet of filo with the short side nearest to you and paint with the butter mixture using the pastry brush.

**5** Place a quarter of the fruit mix in the centre at the nearest end to you using the teaspoon.

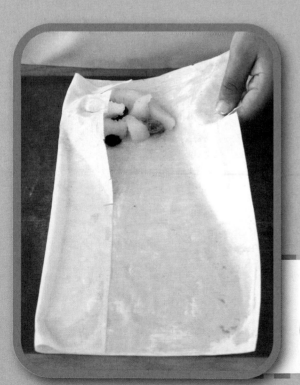

**6** Then fold in the long sides to cover the mixture.

turn the page ▷

▷ continues from page 99

**7** Now dab the filo again with some more of your butter mix then roll up the length of the pastry to make a parcel.

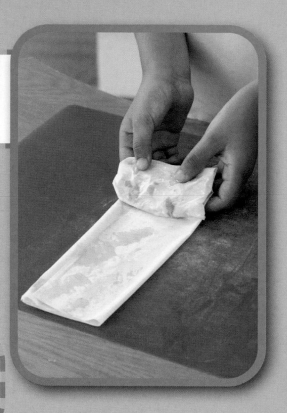

**8** Repeat to make 4 parcels in all and brush the top of the finished parcels with the remaining butter mixture. Put onto the baking tray.

**9** You'll need to ask an adult for help with this part. Put in a preheated oven, 180°C fan, 200°C, Gas Mark 6, and bake for just 10 minutes.

Once the Fruity Filo Parcels have cooled down a little (the filling is very hot!), you can eat them!

# How to fold a filo parcel

**Step 1**

**Step 2**

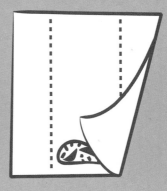

**Step 3**

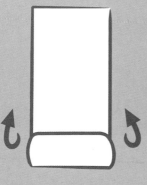

**Step 4**

**Step 5**

## KATY SAYS

Try making the parcels with tinned apples or peaches. These parcels are great in lunch boxes.

Before cooking, wash your hands and put an apron on

# i can cook
# Sweet things

# Gooseberry upside-down loaf

This cake is delicious served in slices with a glass of milk.

## Ingredients:

- vegetable oil for greasing
- ½ cup fresh gooseberries
- 90 g golden caster sugar
- 70 g soft butter
- 70 g wholemeal flour
- 1 teaspoon baking powder
- ½ teaspoon cinnamon
- 1 egg

## Equipment:

- workmat
- cup
- scales
- teaspoon
- pastry brush
- small loaf tin (500 g size)
- baking paper
- kitchen paper or clean tea towel
- scissors
- mixing bowl
- fork
- spatula
- baking tray
- oven glove (for adult use)

**Makes 5–6 slices**

**What to do**

**1** Weigh or measure all the ingredients. Grease a small loaf tin with a little vegetable oil using the pastry brush and line the bottom and 2 sides with a strip of baking paper.

**2** Prepare the gooseberries by washing them and patting them dry on kitchen paper or a clean tea towel. Then top and tail them with the scissors. Sprinkle the bottom of the prepared loaf tin with 20g of golden caster sugar, then place the fresh, whole gooseberries on top.

**3** Put the remaining 70 g golden caster sugar, butter and flour to the bowl. Add the baking powder and cinnamon. Squash all the ingredients together with your fingers until it makes a soft ball of mixture.

**4** Break the egg into a cup and whisk with the fork, then add to the bowl.

**5** Mash the mixture together with the fork until the egg is mixed in, then beat it well with the spatula. Put the mixture in the prepared tin and place on the baking tray.

**6** You'll need to ask an adult for help with this part. Put in a preheated oven, 160°C fan, 180°C, Gas Mark 4, for 25–30 minutes until golden on the top.

Allow to cool before turning out upside down to find the hidden fruit.

**KATY SAYS**

You could use Demerara sugar instead of caster for extra crunch!

# Crumble-topped tarts

Serve these tarts with fresh raspberries or strawberries.

## Ingredients:

- ¼ block shortcrust pastry (125 g)
- 4 rounded teaspoons lemon curd
- 30 g butter
- 2 tablespoons rolled oats
- 2 dessertspoons caster sugar
- 2 tablespoons self-raising flour

## Equipment:

- workmat
- scales
- 2 teaspoons
- tablespoon
- dessertspoon
- large 6-hole muffin tray
- baking tray
- flour dredger
- rolling pin
- 8 cm cutter
- small bowl
- fork
- oven gloves (for adult use)

**Serves 4**

## What to do

**1** Weigh or measure all the ingredients. Put the muffin tray on to the baking tray. Using your dredger, flour your surface with a little flour.

### KATY SAYS

You only need to use a little flour on your surface to stop the pastry sticking.

**2** Roll out the pastry and cut out the bases for your tarts using the cutter. Line four holes in the muffin tray with the pastry circles.

**3** Spoon the lemon curd into the pastry cases – about 1 rounded teaspoon is enough. If you over fill, they boil over and spoil.

**4** Ask an adult to melt the butter in the small bowl and leave it to cool down a little. Next add the oats, sugar and then the flour to the butter, and mix with a fork, breaking it up into crumbs.

**5** Sprinkle the crumbs onto the top of your tarts.

**6** You'll need to ask an adult for help with this part. Put in a preheated oven, 180°C fan, 200°C, Gas Mark 6, for 15–20 minutes.

As soon as the Crumble-topped Tarts have cooled down completely, you can eat them!

# Strawberry crown

Serve this strawberry treat with yogurt or ice cream.

## Ingredients:

- 100 g self-raising flour
- 20 g soft butter
- 1 teaspoon caster sugar
- up to 50 ml warm milk
- 3 large or 6 medium fresh strawberries
- 1 heaped teaspoon red fruit jam (proper jam, not conserve)
- 2–3 fresh basil leaves
- 1 teaspoon Demerara sugar

## Equipment:

- workmat
- scales
- 3 teaspoons
- measuring jug
- mixing bowl
- fork
- flour dredger
- baking tray and paper
- table knife
- oven gloves (for adult use)

**Serves 2**

## What to do

**KATY SAYS**

Put the base on the baking tray before you add your topping.

**1** Weigh or measure all the ingredients. Put the flour and butter together in the bowl and rub them together with your fingers (as if you were tickling the mixture) until you get a fine crumbly mixture.

**2** Add the caster sugar and mix with the fork. Then tip in most of the milk and mix until it starts to stick together. You may not need all the milk.

**3** Sprinkle flour on the workmat using the dredger. Turn the dough out onto the mat and gently make it into a ball, then flatten it with your hands. Make a dip in the middle. Put onto the paper-lined baking tray.

**4** Cut the strawberries in halves with the table knife; bigger ones might need cutting again. Put them to one side.

**5** Using the 2 teaspoons, put the jam into the middle of the dough and spread it out using the back of one teaspoon just like you would if you were making a savoury pizza with tomato.

**6** Tear the basil into small pieces and sprinkle some on top of the jam. Add the strawberries on top of the jam. Finish with the rest of the fresh basil and sprinkle the top with a little Demerara sugar.

**7** You'll need to ask an adult for help with this part. Put in a preheated oven, 200°C fan, 220°C, Gas Mark 7, for 12–15 minutes.

**Once the Strawberry Crown has cooled down a little (the jam can get very hot), you can eat it!**

# Sticky chocolate cake

**Serve with some extra mandarin segments.**

## Ingredients:

- vegetable oil for greasing
- 4 tablespoons rice or soya milk
- 1 teaspoon bicarbonate of soda
- 100 g self-raising flour
- 1 tablespoon cocoa powder
- 4 tablespoons caster sugar
- 25 g soya-based non-dairy spread
- 2 tablespoons runny honey
- 6 –10 mandarin segments, fresh or tinned (well drained)

## Equipment:

- workmat
- scales
- 2 tablespoons
- teaspoon
- pastry brush
- small loaf tin (500 g size)
- cup
- 2 mixing bowls
- wooden spoon
- spatula
- baking tray
- oven gloves (for adult use)

**Makes 5–6 slices**

### What to do

**1** Weigh or measure all the ingredients. Prepare the loaf tin by brushing the vegetable oil on the inside of the tin.

**2** Pour the milk alternative into the cup. Add the bicarbonate of soda and stir with a teaspoon.

**KATY SAYS**

This yummy chocolate cake is dairy free.

**3** In a bowl put the flour and the cocoa together and stir – this is the 'dry' bowl.

**4** In another bowl beat together the sugar, the spread and the runny honey with a wooden spoon until light and fluffy – this is the 'wet' bowl.

**5** Stir the milky mixture again. Now add some of the dry mix to the wet bowl and then add some of the milky mixture to this. Repeat until all the ingredients are in the wet bowl. Now mix together using the wooden spoon until you have a smooth mixture.

**6** Arrange half of the mandarin slices on the bottom of the loaf tin. Put the cake mixture on top of the fruit and arrange the rest on the top. You may want to use a spatula to get all the mixture out. Put the loaf tin on to the baking tray.

**7** You'll need to ask an adult for help with this part. Put in a preheated oven, 170°C fan, 190°C, Gas Mark 5, for 25–30 minutes until risen and springing back from a touch.

**When the Sticky Chocolate Cake has cooled, you can eat it!**

# Baked blackcurrant rice

Serve the rice pudding with a shortbread biscuit.

## Ingredients:

- 250 ml apple juice
- 50 g arborio rice
- 40 g fresh blackcurrants
- 2 tablespoons sugar
- ½ teaspoon vanilla extract

## Equipment:

- workmat
- measuring jug
- scales
- tablespoon
- teaspoon
- ovenproof dish with lid (about 400 ml capacity)
- baking tray
- oven gloves (for adult use)

**Serves 2**

## What to do

**KATY SAYS**

Make sure you remove all the blackcurrant stalks, as they don't taste very nice!

**1** Weigh or measure all the ingredients.

**2** Pour the juice into the ovenproof dish. Add the rice.

**3** Now prepare the blackcurrants by pinching out any woody stalks before adding them to the ovenproof dish.

**4** Add the sugar and the vanilla extract.

**5** Stir with the teaspoon and put on the lid. Place on the baking tray.

**6** You'll need to ask an adult for help with this part. Put in a preheated oven, 200°C fan, 220°C, Gas Mark 7, for 20 minutes, then leave to stand for at least 10 minutes with the lid on (the rice will carry on cooking).

**When the Baked Blackcurrant Rice has cooled a bit, you can eat it!**

# Fruity prize pie

Serve the pie warm or cold with yogurt or ice cream.

## Ingredients:

- 125 g shortcrust pastry
- 2 heaped teaspoons rolled oats
- about 140 g fresh cherries
- 2 heaped tablespoons Demerara sugar
- pinch of cinnamon

## Equipment:

- workmat
- scales
- teaspoon
- tablespoon
- baking tray and paper
- flour dredger
- rolling pin
- plastic bag (18 x 23 cm minimum)
- mixing bowl
- oven gloves (adult use)

**Serves 2**

## What to do

**1** Weigh or measure all the ingredients. Line the baking tray with baking paper.

**2** Using your dredger, flour your surface with a little plain flour. Shape the pastry in your hands into a rough circle (disc) shape. You can turn it on its side and roll it or use the palm of your hands to pat the corners until it is round.

### KATY SAYS

Remember to dispose of the plastic bag carefully.

**3** Using the rolling pin, roll the pastry out. Turn the pastry often so that it stays round. It should be about 5mm thick and about the size of a side plate (about 20 cm across). Put onto the baking tray.

**4** Sprinkle the centre of the pastry with the oats, leaving space all around – like an island of oats – these will soak up the fruit juices!

**5** Pull the stalks off the cherries and put them into the bag. Bash gently with the rolling pin to split them. Tip the cherries into the mixing bowl and pick out the stones – be sure to double check that all the stones have been removed. Add 1 tablespoon of the Demerera sugar and a pinch of cinnamon, then stir.

**6** Put the cherries into the middle of the pastry on top of the oats. Leave an area of pastry free of fruit all the way round the edge. Next brush the edge with leftover juice.

**7** Now using your fingers pinch together the sides of the pie to shape. (You should still be able to see some of the fruit at the top of the pie). Now brush the pastry with the cherry juice again. Sprinkle a little more Demerara sugar on top.

**8** You'll need to ask an adult for help with this part. Put in a preheated oven, 180°C fan, 200°C, Gas Mark 6, for 20–25 minutes. Let it cool on the sheet.

**Once the Fruity Prize Pie has cooled down a little, you can eat it!**

# Pear, ginger & chocolate crumble

Serve the crumble with plain yogurt, vanilla ice cream or custard.

## Ingredients:

- 4 pear halves, fresh or tinned
- 3 tablespoons apple juice
- 2 teaspoons ginger conserve
- 1 tablespoon plain chocolate drops
- 2 dessertspoons Demerera sugar
- 15 g soft butter
- 2 dessertspoons plain flour
- 2 dessertspoons rolled oats

## Equipment:

- workmat
- tablespoon
- teaspoon
- dessertspoon
- scales
- ovenproof dish (about 400 ml capacity)
- mixing bowl
- baking tray
- oven gloves (adult use)

**Serves 2**

## What to do

**1** Weigh or measure all the ingredients. If you are using fresh pears, ask an adult to cut them in half and to take out the core for you.

**2** Arrange the pear halves in your cooking dish cut side up and pour over the apple juice.

### KATY SAYS

You can use big pinches of ground ginger if you haven't got any ginger conserve.

**3** Share out the ginger and most of the chocolate drops between the pear pieces (keep some of the chocolate drops back for the crumble topping). Sprinkle about 1 dessertspoon of the sugar over the fruit.

**4** Now make the crumble topping by putting the sugar with the butter, flour and oats in the mixing bowl and rubbing them between your fingers, like tickling, until you make fine crumbs. Add the remaining chocolate drops and mix well.

**5** Sprinkle the crumble topping all over the pears. Put the ovenproof dish onto the baking tray.

**6** You'll need to ask an adult for help with this part. Put in a preheated oven, 180°c fan, 200°C, Gas Mark 6, for 20–25 minutes until the pears are soft, the top is golden and the chocolate has melted.

When the Pear, Ginger & Chocolate Crumble has cooled down a bit, you can eat it!

# Strawberry meringue pudding

Serve the pudding with plain yogurt or ice cream.

## Ingredients:

- 3–4 sponge fingers
- around 200 g strawberries or any mixed red fruits (either fresh or tinned)
- 1 large egg
- 2 tablespoons caster sugar

## Equipment:

- workmat
- scales
- tablespoon
- ovenproof dish (about 400ml capacity)
- baking tray
- fork
- cup
- 2 mixing bowls
- whisk
- spatula
- oven gloves (for adult use)

**Serves 2–4**

## What to do

**1** Weigh or measure all the ingredients. Put the ovenproof dish onto the baking tray before you start.

**2** First put the sponge fingers in the bottom of the dish – this is going to make the base of your pudding.

**3** Now, if using fresh fruit, prepare in a mixing bowl by squashing it using the back of a fork to release the juice and then add all of it (and juices) to the dish. If using tinned, drain off the juice add all the fruit and add about 4–5 tablespoons of the juice to the dish.

**4** Now separate the egg yolk from the white by breaking the egg into a cup then pouring the egg through your fingers over a bowl, catching the yolk. Use the yolk in another recipe.

**5** Whisk the white until it becomes a frothy white foam and begins to hold its shape, then continue whisking and adding the sugar a little at a time until it forms stiff peaks. Pile the meringue on top of the fruit, using the spatula, and hide the fruit layer.

**6** You'll need to ask an adult for help with this part. Put in a preheated oven, 210°C fan, 220°C, Gas Mark 7, for 6–8 minutes or until the topping is golden and crispy.

**KATY SAYS**

Hold the yolk gently when you are pouring the egg through your fingers.

When the Strawberry Meringue Pudding has cooled a little, you can eat it!

# Celebration cornet cakes

Serve the cakes with extra fresh raspberries.

## Ingredients:

- 1 egg
- 2 tablespoons vegetable oil
- 2 tablespoons milk
- ½ teaspoon vanilla extract
- 3 tablespoons fresh raspberries
- ½ cup (60 g) self-raising flour
- 1 tablespoon caster sugar
- 3 flat-bottomed ice cream cup cornets

## Equipment:

- workmat
- scales
- tablespoon
- 2 teaspoons
- cup
- 2 mixing bowls
- fork
- small loaf tin (500 g size)
- baking tray
- oven gloves (for adult use)

**What to do**

Makes 3

**1** Weigh and measure all the ingredients.

**2** Break the egg into the cup, then separate the egg by making a claw shape with one hand and pour through the whole egg and catch the yolk. Put the white into a bowl (and use the yolk in another recipe). Whisk with the fork to make some bubbles. Add the oil and milk and mix again. Then add the vanilla extract.

**3** Take 6 raspberries and put them on one side. Add the remaining raspberries to the wet mixture.

**4** Put the flour to the second mixing bowl, then add the sugar.

**5** Tip the wet ingredients into the flour bowl and stir the ingredients together with a tablespoon until completely mixed. The mixture will be quite wet.

**6** Put the cup cornets into the loaf tin so they stand up straight. Add a raspberry to the bottom of each cornet. Then scoop and slide the mixture into the cup cornets using the 2-spoon method and add one raspberry on the top of each.

**7** Place on the baking tray. You'll need to ask an adult for help with this part. Put in a preheated oven, 180°C fan, 200°C, Gas Mark 6, for 20–25 minutes. Leave to cool.

### KATY SAYS

If you crush the raspberries in the wet mixture, your cake mixture will turn pink!

**When the Celebration Cornet Cakes have cooled a little, you can eat one!**

# Fruit jumble

Serve this fruity pudding with yogurt or custard.

## Ingredients:

- 2–3 fresh ripe plums
- 1 tablespoon orange juice
- 1 tablespoon runny honey
- 40 g butter
- 1 thick slice bread
- 1 tablespoon Demerara sugar

## Equipment:

- workmat
- tablespoon
- scales
- ovenproof dish (about 400ml capacity)
- baking tray
- table knife
- mixing bowl
- fork
- oven gloves (for adult use)

**Serves 2**

### What to do

**1** Weigh or measure all the ingredients. Place the ovenproof dish on the baking tray.

**2** Take your knife for a walk around the plum then twist the plums in half. Take out the stones.

**KATY SAYS**

The sprinkled Demerara sugar will give the bread a crunchy top.

**3** Lay the plums flat-side down on the mat and cut them again, this will make 4 pieces – called quarters. Put them into the ovenproof dish. Add the orange juice and honey and stir together.

**4** Melt the butter in the mixing bowl – you will need an adult to help you with this. Put to one side to cool down while you cut the bread into large squares with the table knife to make the topping. When the butter is cool enough, drop the bread into the butter and swish it around to coat the bread. Add some of the Demerara sugar in, too, and mix up with the fork.

**5** Tip the bread topping on top of the fruit and sprinkle the top with the leftover Demerara sugar.

**6** You'll need to ask an adult for help with this part. Put the dish in a preheated oven at 180°C fan, 200°C, Gas Mark 6, for 20–25 minutes or until the topping is golden and crispy and the fruit soft.

When the Fruit Jumble has cooled a little, you can eat it!

# Katy's courgette cake

Serve in slices with some fresh fruit such as strawberries.

## Ingredients:

- vegetable oil for greasing
- 50 g soft brown sugar
- 50 g soft butter
- 1 egg
- 90 g self-raising flour
- 1 teaspoon mixed spice
- half a lime
- 60 g courgette

## Equipment:

- workmat
- scales
- teaspoon
- small loaf tin (500 g size)
- pastry brush
- mixing bowl
- fork
- cup
- wooden spoon
- grater
- baking tray
- oven gloves (for adult use)

**Makes 1 loaf (5–6 slices)**

## What to do

**1** Weigh or measure all the ingredients. Brush the loaf tin with oil using the pastry brush.

**2** Put the sugar and butter into the mixing bowl. Squish the ingredients together with the back of the fork until completely combined.

**3** Break the egg into the cup and whisk with the fork. Add to the bowl and stir with the wooden spoon. Add the flour and mixed spice and stir again.

**4** To add the lime juice, squeeze the lime half with your hands over the bowl. Mix up really well again.

**5** Grate the courgette. Add this to the mixture and beat well with the wooden spoon. Then put the mixture into the loaf tin. Put the loaf tin on to the baking tray.

**6** You'll need to ask an adult for help with this part. Put the dish in a preheated oven at 200°C fan, 220°C, Gas Mark 7, for 20–25 minutes or until golden on the top.

### KATY SAYS

The grated courgette will make the cake lovely and moist.

**When Katy's Courgette Cake has cooled down a little, you can eat it!**

# Index

apples
  chunky cheese loaf 80–1
  crunchy coleslaw 64–5

bacon
  playtime popovers 86–7
baked blackcurrant rice 112–13
baked explorer pancakes 68–9
basil
  pepper boats 76–7
  treasure chest tart 66–7
bees 17, 46
birds 17
biscuits
  cheese and tomato melts 82–3
  fig and fudge biscuits 88–9
blackcurrants
  baked blackcurrant rice 112–13
blueberries
  growing 22–3
bread
  chicken in a basket 56–7
  chunky cheese loaf 80–1
  fruit jumble 122–3
  seaside bites 58–9
buns, spiced fun 92–3
butter
  baked potatoes with herby butter 62–3

cabbage
  crunchy coleslaw 64–5
cakes
  celebration cornet cakes 120–1
  gooseberry upside down loaf 104–5
  Katy's courgette cake 124–5
  picnic parkin 94–5
  spiced parsnip cake 96–7
  sticky chocolate cake 110–11
  strawberry crown 108–9
carrots
  crunchy coleslaw 64–5
  growing 36–7
  sunny carrot cake 90–1
celebration cornet cakes 120–1

cheese
  cheese and tomato melts 82–3
  cheesy pasta rolls 52–3
  chunky cheese loaf 80–1
  green parcel pie 74–5
  melon & feta cheese salad with
   redcurrants 70–1
  mini cheese munchies 84–5
  pepper boats 76–7
cherries
  fruity prize pie 114–15
chicken
  chicken in a basket 56–7
  scrunchy crunchy chicken 50–1
chocolate
  pear, ginger and chocolate crumble
   116–17
  sticky chocolate cake 110–11
chunky cheese loaf 80–1
coleslaw, crunchy 64–5
coriander
  falafel footballs 72–3
courgettes
  green parcel pie 74–5
  growing 34–5
  Katy's courgette cake 124–5
cream
  scrunchy crunchy chicken 50–1
crumble, pear, ginger and chocolate
  116–17
crumble topped tarts 106–7
crunchy coleslaw 64–5
cup measures 10
currants
  spiced fun buns 92–3

eggs, breaking 11

falafel footballs 72–3
fast growing plants 15
feeding plants 16
fig and fudge biscuits 88–9
filo pastry
  folding a filo parcel 101

fruity filo parcels 98–101
green parcel pie 74–5
scrunchy crunchy chicken 50–1
fish
  haddock puff 60–1
  seaside bites 58–9
French beans
  growing 26–7
fruit jumble 122–3
fruity filo parcels 98–101
fruity prize pie 114–15
fudge
  fig and fudge biscuits 88–9

gardening 7–9, 12–47
  blueberries 22–3
  carrots 36–7
  courgettes 34–5
  French beans 26–7
  fun pots 40
  lunchbox plants 32–3
  magic name pots 18–19
  mint 42–3
  pests 17
  plants
   fast growing 15
   feeding 16
   slow growing 15
   smelly 41
   watering 16
  potatoes 38–9
  radishes 24–5
  safety 9
  salad leaves 30–1
  sowing seeds 14–15
  strawberries 20–1
  sunflowers 41
  thyme 44–5
  tomatoes 28–9
  wildlife 17, 40
  edible wildlife garden 46–7
garlic
  baked potatoes with herby butter 62–3
  falafel footballs 72–3

ginger
  pear, ginger and chocolate crumble 116–17
gooseberry upside down loaf 104–5
golden syrup
  picnic parkin 94–5
grapes
  chicken in a basket 56–7
graters 10
green beans
  baked explorer pancakes 68–9
green parcel pie 74–5

haddock puff 60–1
hand washing song 11
herbs
  baked potatoes with herby butter 62–3
honey
  fruit jumble 122–3
  sticky chocolate cake 110–11

Katy's courgette cake 124–5
kidney beans
  falafel footballs 72–3
knives 10

ladybirds 17, 46
lasagne
  cheesy pasta rolls 52–3
lemon curd
  crumble topped tarts 106–7
liquids, measuring 11
lunch 48–77
  baked explorer pancakes 68–9
  baked potatoes with herby butter 62–3
  cheesy pasta rolls 52–3
  chicken in a basket 56–7
  crunchy coleslaw 64–5
  falafel footballs 72–3
  green parcel pie 74–5
  haddock puff 60–1
  melon & feta cheese salad with redcurrants 70–1
  pepper boats 76–7
  scrunchy crunchy chicken 50–1
  seaside bites 58–9
  treasure chest tart 66–7
  turkey snaps 54–5
lunchbox plants 32–3

magic name pots 18–19
mandarins
  sticky chocolate cake 110–11

measuring 10
  liquids 11
melon & feta cheese salad with redcurrants 70–1
meringue
  strawberry meringue pudding 118–19
mini cheese munchies 84–5
mint
  growing 42–3
mixed spice
  fruity filo parcels 98–101
  Katy's courgette cake 124–5
  spiced fun buns 92–3
  spiced parsnip cake 96–7
mixing bowls 10
  'wet' and 'dry' bowls 11
muffins
  playtime popovers 86–7
mushrooms
  playtime popovers 86–7

pancakes, baked explorer 68–9
parkin, picnic 94–5
parsnips
  spiced parsnip cake 96–7
pasta
  cheesy pasta rolls 52–3
pears
  fruity filo parcels 98–101
  pear, ginger and chocolate crumble 116–17
peppers
  pepper boats 76–7
  popping 11
  treasure chest tart 66–7
pests 17
picnic parkin 94–5
pie, fruity prize 114–15
pineapple
  sunny carrot cake 90–1
pine nuts
  pepper boats 76–7
playtime popovers 86–7
plums
  fruit jumble 122–3
polenta
  mini cheese munchies 84–5
potatoes
  baked potatoes with herby butter 62–3
  growing 38–9
  making potato prints 41
puff pastry
  haddock puff 60–1
  treasure chest tart 66–7

pumpkin seeds
  spiced parsnip cake 96–7

radishes
  growing 24–5
raisins
  crunchy coleslaw 64–5
raspberries
  celebration cornet cakes 120–1
  crumble topped tarts 106–7
redcurrants
  melon & feta cheese salad with redcurrants 70–1
rice
  baked blackcurrant rice 112–13

safety in the garden 9
salads
  growing salad leaves 30–1
  melon & feta cheese salad with redcurrants 70–1
scales 10
scissors 9, 10
scrunchy crunchy chicken 50–1
seaside bites 58–9
slow growing plants 15
smoked haddock
  haddock puff 60–1
sowing seeds 14–15
spiced fun buns 92–3
spiced parsnip cake 96–7
spinach
  cheesy pasta rolls 52–3
  mini cheese munchies 84–5
sponge fingers
  strawberry meringue pudding 118–19
spoons 10
  two spoon method 11
sticky chocolate cake 110–11
strawberries
  crumble topped tarts 106–7
  plants 20–1
  strawberry crown 108–9
  strawberry meringue pudding 118–19
sunflowers 41
sunny carrot cake 90–1
sweetcorn
  baked explorer pancakes 68–9
  treasure chest tart 66–7
sweet things 102–25
  baked blackcurrant rice 112–13
  celebration cornet cakes 120–1
  crumble topped tarts 106–7
  fruit jumble 122–3
  fruity prize pie 114–15

gooseberry upside down loaf 104–5
Katy's courgette cake 124–5
pear, ginger and chocolate crumble
    116–17
sticky chocolate cake 110–11
strawberry crown 108–9
strawberry meringue pudding
    118–19

tarts, crumble topped 106–7
tea 78–101
    cheese and tomato melts 82–3
    chunky cheese loaf 80–1
    fig and fudge biscuits 88–9
    fruity filo parcels 98–101
    mini cheese munchies 84–5

picnic parkin 94–5
playtime popovers 86–7
spiced fun buns 92–3
spiced parsnip cake 96–7
sunny carrot cake 90–1
thyme 44–5
tickling 11
tip and load 11
tomatoes
    growing 28–9
    pepper boats 76–7
    playtime popovers 86–7
    reasure chest tart 66–7
tomato juice
    cheese and tomato melts 82–3
topping and tailing 11

treasure chest tart 66–7
trout
    seaside bites 58–9
turkey snaps 54–5

walnuts
    spiced parsnip cake 96–7
    sunny carrot cake 90–1
watercress
    haddock puff 60–1
watering plants 16
wildlife 17, 40
    edible wildlife garden 46–7
window boxes 46–7
work surfaces 10

# Acknowledgements

**Thank you to the children who cooked and gardened for the photography:**
Jemima Baker, Travis Beckey, Esme Benson, Kitty Betteridge, Monty Betteridge, Elijah Bouchier, Ocean Brobbey, Caitlin Dennis, William Dennis, Elizabeth Denton, Ryan Duong, Daniel Ellis, James Ellis, Nya Enver, Ruby-Rose Ferreira, Mylea Geal, Evie Gibson, Florence Hampton, Jessica Hawkins, Lily Hawkins , Harlan Hines, Charlotte Honer, Nathan Kemp, Sienna Kemp, Rose Lemon, Maya Lozzi, Jack Mercer, Grace Nunn, Dylan Rose, Mia Rose, Henry Spicer, Kacey Swaffield, Max Thompson, Millie Wakefield, Jessica Wilton

**Thank you also** to Vegetable Plants Direct (www.vegetableplantsdirect.co.uk) for the plants and Mr Fothergill's Direct (www.mr-fothergills.co.uk) for the seeds and Horwood for the Judge multi purpose grater.

**All photography** is by Vanessa Davies for Octopus Publishing with the exception of the following:

**Alamy** Ace Stock Ltd 40 below; Bon Appetit 25 below; Botany Focus 27 below; Elly Godfroy 37 below; Johner Images 39 below, Nigel Cattlin 31 below.
**Getty Images** Barbara Buchner 41 below; Carol Sharp/Flower Photos 14 right.

**Executive Producer:** Christopher Pilkington
**Presenter**: Katy Ashworth
**Katy Ashworth's Agent:** Jan Croxson
**Literary Agent:** Amanda Preston
**Paralegal:** Penny Roberts
**Endemol Worldwide Brands, Regional Director UK:** Seema Khan
**Licensing Manager:** Nicole Sloman

**Managing Editor:** Clare Churly
**Deputy Art Director:** Yasia Williams-Leedham
**Designer:** Miranda Harvey
**Photographer:** Vanessa Davies
**Home Economist:** Denise Smart
**Stylist:** Isabel de Cordova
**Picture Research:** Giulia Hetherington
**Production Manager:** Peter Hunt